ENCYCLOPAEDIA OF INDIAN GOVERNMENT: PROGRAMMES AND POLICIES

ENCYCLOPAEDIA
OF
INDIAN GOVERNMENT:
PROGRAMMES AND POLICIES

Vol. 37

Space Research

Edited by

Satish Tiwari

ANMOL PUBLICATIONS PVT. LTD.
NEW DELHI - 110 002 (INDIA)

ANMOL PUBLICATIONS PVT. LTD.
4374/4B, Ansari Road, Daryaganj
New Delhi - 110 002

Encyclopaedia of Indian Government: Programmes and Policies

First Edition, 2000
ISBN 81-261-0515-1 (Set)

[Responsibility for the facts stated, opinions expressed, conclusions reached and plagiarism, if any, in these volumes is entirely that of the Editor. The Publisher bears no responsibility for them whatsoever.]

PRINTED IN INDIA

Published by J.L. Kumar for Anmol Publications Pvt. Ltd., New Delhi - 110 002 and Printed at Mehra Offset Press, Delhi.

Contents

Preface v

1. Introduction 1
2. Organisation 8
3. Space Applications 15
4. Important Projects and Technology Development 69
5. Space Sciences 100
6. Sponsored Research 175
7. Space Industry Partnership 178
8. Cooperation 184
9. Publications and Public Relations 211
10. Space in Parliament 216
11. General 218

Preface

Encyclopaedia of Indian Government: Programmes and Policies contains authoritative information on about fifty departmental policies and their future developmental programmes.

Organised to be completed in 40 volumes, this gigantic work covers Agriculture; Atomic Energy; Chemicals and Fertilizers; Coal; Commerce; Communication; Culture; Defence; Education; Environment and Forests; External Affairs; Finance; Food & Consumer Affairs; Food Processing Industries; Health and Family Welfare; Home Affairs and Internal Security; Human Resources; Industry; Information and Broadcasting; Labour; Law, Justice and Company Affairs; Non-conventional Energy Sources; Ocean Development; Parliamentary Affairs; Personnel, Public Grievances and Pensions; Petroleum and Natural Gas; Planning and Programme Implementation; Planning and Statistics; Posts and Telegraphs; Power; Rural Development; Science and Technology; Social Justice and Empowerment; Space; States Affairs; Steel; Steel and Mines; Sugar and Edible Oils; Surface Transport; Textiles; Tourism; Urban Development; Water Resources; Women and Child development etc.

Based on the information derived from authoritative sources, this work contains authentic facts and figures. I am deeply beholden to all the scholars whose writings are cited or substantially made use of in the present work. I am also thankful to Anmol Publications Pvt. Ltd. for undertaking publication of this encyclopaedia. I am solely responsible for shortcomings in presentation of matter.

Encyclopaedic in nature, this will prove a dependable reference work for scholars and academics besides those appearing for different competitive examinations.

—**Satish Tiwari**

1

Introduction

One of the major strides that India has taken since independence is in the field of space. It is significant that, today, the country has established a viable, self-reliant space programme that is precisely tuned towards national developmental tasks. Making a modest beginning in 1963 with the launch of a small sounding rocket from Thumba, near Thiruvananthapuram, India has come a long way in establishing space systems like Indian National Satellite (INSAT) and Indian Remote Sensing (IRS) satellite systems that form a crucial element of the national infrastructure for telecommunication, television broadcasting, meteorology, resources survey and management. Both INSAT and IRS satellites are now designed and built indigenously. Further, India has designed, developed and operationalised the Polar Satellite Launch Vehicle, PSLV, for launching IRS class of satellites and, soon, will be able to launch INSAT class of satellites also with the development of Geosynchronous Satellite Launch Vehicle (GSLV).

The Indian Remote Sensing Satellite (IRS) system comprises a constellation of four satellites, including IRS-1C and IRS-1D which are considered as world's best civilian remote sensing satellites. IRS system continues to provide remote sensing services. Data from these satellites have been put to several important applications

-agricultural crop acreage and yield estimation, ground water targeting, forest survey, identification of wasteland for possible reclamation, snow-melt run-off estimates, irrigation command area management, mineral prospecting, identification of potential fishing zones, urban planning, environment monitoring and other applications.

The unique capabilities of remote sensing satellites have enabled India to take up Integrated Mission for Sustainable Development (IMSD) which has made substantial progress during the year in generating locale-specific plans for land and water resources development as well as taking up implementation of the recommended plans. The high spatial resolution data from IRS-1C and IRSû1D have found new applications in the areas of urban sprawl mapping, infrastructure planning and other large scale thematic mapping. A project on Forecasting Agricultural output using Space, Agro meteorology and Land observation (FASAL) has been initiated with the implementation of pilot study in Orissa. A project to characterise the bio-diversity at landscape level using remote sensing and geographic information system data basis is another important application of remote sensing initiated during the year.

India continues to derive commercial benefits from its IRS satellites. Data from IRS satellites is now acquired and used by several countries including those in North America, Europe, Thailand, Japan, Korea and Dubai, under commercial agreements. In all, about ten stations world over are expected to receive the data in the near future.

Substantial progress has been made in the development and fabrication of the follow-on satellites in IRS series, namely, IRS-P4 (OCEANSAT) carrying sophisticated instruments like Ocean Colour Monitor and

Multi Frequency Scanning Microwave Radiometer which will provide valuable information on ocean biological parameters, sea surface temperature, atmospheric water vapour content and sea surface winds. The satellite is planned for launch in 1999-2000 on board India's Polar Satellite Launch Vehicle (PSLV). Work on IRS-P5 (CARTOSAT) which will provide high resolution stereo images for cartographic applications and digital terrain modelling has also progressed well and this satellite is planned for launch during 2000-01, also, on board PSLV. Configuration of the follow-on satellites, IRS-P6 (RESOURCESAT), is also being finalised and it will be launched by PSLV during 2001-02 to continue and enhance the services provided at present by IRS-1C and IRS-1D.

INSAT system is one of the largest domestic communication satellite systems in the world today with five satellites, three of them - INSAT-2A, INSAT-2B and INSAT-2C - built indigenously. The other satellites are the last of the first generation satellite INSAT-1D and, INSAT-2DT that was acquired from ARABSAT Organisation to augment the INSAT system. During the year, seven high power C-band transponders have also been leased from a Thailand satellite, THAICOM-3 to further augment the INSAT capacity

INSAT continues to provide telecommunications, television broadcasting, radio networking, meteorology and disaster management services. With a view to emphasise the importance of using space technology for grassroots level applications, a two year pilot project, Jhabua Development Communications Project (JDCP), was started in November 1996 covering 150 villages. JDCP has been further extended and it is planned to expand the project to cover an additional 462 sites in Jhabua and also add 200 DRS terminals in the adjacent districts of Dhar and Barwani in Madhya Pradesh. The use of Training and Developmental Communication Channel (TDCC) of INSAT continues to grow and more agencies are using this system. There are about 375 receivers set up by various agencies for using this network.

INSAT system is expected to get a substantial boost in 1999-2000 with the commissioning of INSAT-2E and the planned launches of first two satellites, INSAT-3A and INSAT-3B, under the five-satellite INSAT-3 series. Launch of INSAT-3B is being advanced to precede that of INSAT-3A in order to meet, expeditiously, the requirement of extended C-band transponder capacity. Work on follow-on satellites in the INSAT-3 series has also been initiated during the year.

INSAT-2E is awaiting launch by an Ariane launch vehicle from Kourou in French Guyana. INSAT-2E will carry 17 transponders and meteorological instrument, Very High Resolution Radiometer (VHRR) similar to that of INSAT-2A and INSAT-2B but with capability to take measurements in the water vapour channel also. It will also carry a charge coupled device camera for the first time in the INSAT series. An equivalent of eleven 36 MHz C-band transponders capacity from this satellite is being leased to International Telecommunication Satellite Organisation, INTELSAT, under a commercial agreement.

With PSLV having become operational with the successful launch of IRS-1D, in September 1997, all future IRS satellites are planned to be launched by this vehicle. The vehicle is now offered to launch satellites of other countries as well. A beginning has already been made; along with Indian Remote Sensing satellite, IRS-P4, PSLV-C2 will be used to launch two small satellites - the Korean KITSAT and the German TUBSAT as piggyback payloads. Another small satellite, PROBA of Belgium, is also booked for launch by PSLV An agreement has been entered into, during the year, with the European launch services provider, Arianespace, to evolve a common satellite interface so that, small satellites could be launched by either PSLV or Ariane.

Substantial progress has been made in the development of India's Geosynchronous Satellite Launch Vehicle, GSLV, during the year; qualification of liquid propulsion strap-on stage and arrival of the first flight cryogenic upper stage from Russia have been major events. The first developmental test flight of GSLV is planned in 1999-2000 and it will be used for launching an experimental satellite, GSAT-1.

India continues to involve industries in executing its space programme, both for tapping the resources with the industries and help the industries to upgrade their technological skills as well as commercialise some of the technologies which are developed for the space programme. Additional licenses have been given during the year to use some of the technologies which have been transferred to industries in view of growing demands for the end products. Several more technologies are in the pipeline for transfer to industries.

Interaction with academic and research laboratories has been further strengthened by farming out several research activities to them, thus, utilising their expertise. Space technology cells and space science and education cells at reputed institutions continue to take up more projects under sponsored research programme.

The X-ray astronomy payload on IRS-P3 satellite continues to provide interesting scientific data on celestial X-ray sources which are being analysed by scientists. The Modular Opto-Electronic Scanner of Germany which is also incorporated on this satellite has been providing data that finds several applications in ocean remote sensing. Few more gamma ray bursts have been detected by SROSS-C2 satellite of India which are being analysed. India continues to participate actively in international science campaigns; the second phase of the Indian Ocean Experiment (INDOEX) commenced in January 1999 with several measurements being made using balloon, rocket, aircraft, satellite and ship-borne instruments. INDOEX is expected to lead to a better understanding of global change phenomenon and improve the present global warming models. Several research projects have been undertaken as part of international Geosphere, Biosphere Programme. Indian sounding rockets have been used to fly scientific instruments of other space agencies for upper atmospheric research. India has developed a cryogenic sampler instrument which has been successfully flown using Balloons for trace gas measurements.

As Chairman, India hosted the 12th Plenary of the international Committee on Earth Observation Satellites in Bangalore during November 1998. India will host the second ESCAP Ministerial Conference on Space Applications in December 1999 at New Delhi. The UN sponsored Centre for Space Science Technology Education established by India continues to offer post-graduate courses in remote sensing, satellite communication, space sciences and satellite meteorology to students from ESCAP countries; the third course on remote sensing has started in October 1998. Several activities have been pursued under cooperative agreements that India has entered into with several space agencies.

India continues to derive commercial benefits from its space capabilities. Lease of transponders to INTELSAT, increasing number of stations worldwide receiving and processing data from IRS satellites, agreements to launch small satellites of other countries using PSLV, increasing number of telemetry and tracking supports provided by Indian TTC network to satellites of other space agencies as well as supply of a few satellite hardware to international space industries show the recognition that India is getting in the competitive international space market.

Thus we have emerged as a front-ranking space-faring nation today with a well-integrated space programme. The planned launches of follow-on satellites in the IRS and INSAT series indicate that India will continue to play a major role in the coming years too. With PSLV already in service and GSLV developmental test flights planned in the near future, the Indian space programme is poised to become fully self-reliant in meeting the national space services.

2

Organisation

The subject of the space research was initially allocated to the Department of Atomic Energy (DAE) in August 1961. In 1962, the Indian National Committee for Space Research (INCOSPAR) was formed by DAE, and in 1969, INCOSPAR was reconstituted under the Indian National Science

Academy and a new organisation, Indian Space Research Organisation was formed under DAE. The national space programme was formally organised in June 1972 with the setting up of Space Commission and the Department of Space (DOS) and Indian Space Research Organisation (ISRO) to promote the development and application of space technology and space science for the socioeconomic benefit of the nation.

DOS implements the policies framed by the Space Commission. Research and development activities are carried out through the Indian Space Research Organisation (ISRO), the National Remote Sensing Agency (NRSA), the Physical Research Laboratory (PRL), the National Mesosphere-Stratosphere-Troposphere Radar Facility (NMRF) and other agencies. Two main national space systems that have been established, namely, the Indian National Satellite (INSAT) system and National Natural Resources Management System (NNRMS) are coordinated and managed by the Secretary-level INSAT

Coordination Committee (ICC) and the Planning Committee of NNRMS (PC-NNRMS), respectively. These committees provide guidelines for evaluation of the systems and also oversee the progress. NNRMS Standing Committees (NNRMS-SC), set up with user ministries and departments, ensure an efficient and coordinated functioning of different NNRMS elements. An Advisory Committee on Space Sciences (ADCOS) guides the research programmes in the area of space science. The Antrix Corporation Limited, Bangalore, established in 1992, is a wholly-owned Government of India company for commercial marketing space products and services.

The Secretariat of DOS and the Headquarters of ISRO are located in Bangalore. The overall coordination of the space programme is carried out by programme offices of ISRO Headquarters in different areas like satellite communication, earth observation systems, launch vehicle programme, space science, technology transfer and industry coordination, international cooperation, publications and public relations and, budget and economic analysis. The major establishments of DOS are as follows:

Vikram Sarabhai Space Centre (VSSC)

VSSC at Thiruvananthapuram is the lead centre for all rocket and launch vehicle programmes. The research and development activities are carried out in the areas of avionics, aeronautics, materials, mechanical engineering, solid propulsion, composites, propellants, polymers and chemicals, launch vehicle, computer and information and systems reliability. A programme planning and evaluation group helps in realising the objectives in a timely and cost effective manner. The research and test facilities are located, mainly, in Thumba and Valiamala. The composite development activities are carried out at Vattiyoorkavu in Thiruvananthapuram. An Ammonium Perchlorate Experimental Plant has been set up at Aluva.

The Space Physics Laboratory located at Thumba, carries out research in atmospheric and related space sciences.

ISRO Satellite Centre (ISAC)

ISAC at Bangalore is the lead centre for satellite technology. The research and development activities carried in this centre cover digital systems, power systems, communications, microwave, spacecraft assembly and testing, structures, thermal, spacecraft mechanisms, control, spacecraft mission and, computers and information. The centre has fabrication and test facilities for the various activities. The centre also has a programme planning and evaluation group and systems reliability group. The technical physics division at ISAC conducts space science research.

The Laboratory for Electro-Optic Sensors (LEOS), working under the overall umbrella of ISAC, carries out research and development in the field of electro-optic sensors and systems required for satellites.

SHAR centre

SHAR Centre, located at Sriharikota island about 100 km north of Chennai, is the main launch centre of ISRO. In addition, the centre has facilities for processing solid propellant motors required for launch vehicles and their ground testing. The activities in the range operations comprise mission analysis and range safety, programme management, computer facilities, meteorology and range instrumentation. The solid propellant space booster plant processes solid propellants. The liquid propellant storage and service facilities and vehicle assembly and static test facilities are the other two main components of the centre. Quality and reliability group and programme planning and evaluation group provide necessary support to the centre. Sriharikota Common Facilities (SCF) looks after engineering maintenance, transport, fire services, medical and public health, etc. SHAR operates launch ranges at Thumba in Kerala besides the one at Sriharikota, for conducting sounding rocket flights for scientific studies.

SHAR Centre is the lead centre for setting up a second launch pad there for meeting the requirements of future launch vehicles of ISRO.

Liquid Propulsion Systems Centre (LPSC)

LPSC is responsible for the development of liquid Propulsion stages for launch vehicles and auxiliary propulsion systems for both launch vehicles and satellites. All design and development activities relating to liquid propulsion stages, cryogenic propulsion stages and control systems for launch vehicles and spacecraft are carried out at Valiamala, Thiruvananthapuram. The test facilities are located at Mahendragiri in Tamil Nadu. Precision fabrication facilities, development of transducers and integration of satellite propulsion systems are carried out at Bangalore.

Space Applications Centre (SAC)

SAC, Ahmedabad, conducts space applications research and development. The centre has two main areas of research and development, namely, satellite communication and remote sensing for earth resource application including microwave remote sensing. The centre has set up facilities for mechanical fabrication, electronic fabrication including microwave integrated circuits; spacecraft payload fabrication and environmental tests. It has also reliability and quality assurance group and programme planning and project groups. SAC is responsible for the operation of Delhi Earth Station (DES) for satellite communication.

Development and Educational Communication Unit (DECU)

DECU, Ahmedabad, is involved in the conception, definition, planning, implementation and socio-economic evaluation of space applications. DECU works closely with users to experiment innovative space system configurations to meet specific requirements.

The primary functions of DECU include organising space application experiments/ demonstrations, providing communication support for application projects, production of video programmes for education and development, training of TV programme production personnel and social science research in application areas on the society-technology interface.

ISRO Telemetry, Tracking and Command Network (ISTRAC)

ISTRAC has the prime responsibility to provide mission support to near-earth satellites and launch vehicle missions. An integrated network of ground stations at Bangalore, Lucknow, Port Blair, Sriharikota, Thiruvananthapuram, Bearslake and Mauritius has been established by ISTRAC with a multi-mission Spacecraft Control Centre at Bangalore. ISTRAC, which has its headquarters at Bangalore carries out network operations including maintenance of TTC stations and spacecraft operations including scheduling and control of spacecraft. ISTRAC is also in charge of operation of the Local User Terminal/Mission Control Centre (LUT/MCC) under the international programme for satellite-aided search and rescue.

INSAT Master Control Facility (MCF)

MCF located at Hassan in Karnataka is responsible for all the post-launch operations on INSAT satellites including orbit manoeuvres, station keeping and on-orbit operation of the spacecraft. INSAT MCF closely interacts with user agencies for payload operations, setting transponder gains, planning eclipse load shedding station keeping manoeuvres and undertake recovery procedures in case of loss of lock. The MCF is an integrated facility consisting of five satellite control earth stations with associated electronics and a Spacecraft Control Centre for carrying out the satellite control operations.

ISRO Inertial Systems Unit (IISU)

IISU, Thiruvananthapuram, carries out research and development related to inertial sensors and systems required by satellites and launch vehicles.

IISU is organised into research and development divisions in the fields of- navigation systems, satellite inertial systems, bearing and space tribology and inertial systems integration and simulation. Facilities for precision fabrication, assembly, integration and testing have been established.

National Remote Sensing Agency (NRSA)

NRSA at Hyderabad is an autonomous institution supported by DOS. The agency is responsible for acquisition, processing and distribution of data from remote sensing satellites. NRSA has set up the satellite earth-station at Shadnagar, near Hyderabad, for reception of data from Indian remote sensing satellites, US LANDSAT and NOAA, French SPOT and microwave data from the European remote sensing satellite, ERS. It is also engaged in executing various remote sensing application projects in collaboration with the users. NRSA is in charge of the Indian Institute of Remote Sensing at Dehradun.

Physical Research Laboratory (PRL)

PRL, Ahmedabad, is a premier national centre for research in space and allied sciences. It is an autonomous institution supported, mainly, by DOS. It is also entrusted with the management of the Udaipur Solar Observatory (USO). The research programmes of PRL are carried out mainly in four areas, namely, astronomy and astrophysics, planetary atmosphere and aeronomy, earth sciences and solar system studies and theoretical physics.

National Mesosphere-Stratosphere-Troposphere Radar Facility (NMRF)

NMRF is a national facility set up at Gadanki near Tirupati. NMRF is an autonomous society. The facility is available for national and international scientists to conduct atmospheric research.

Antrix corporation limited

The Antrix Corporation Limited located at Antariksh Complex in Bangalore is the apex marketing agency under the Department of Space with access to resources of ISRO as well as the Indian space industry. Antrix markets subsystems and components for satellites, fabricates satellites to user specifications, provides launch services and tracking facilities and also undertakes training of manpower and software development.

3

Space Applications

Indian Space Programme is primarily application driven. The two major space systems have been established under DOS - Indian National Satellite system (INSAT) providing services for telecommunications, television broadcasting and meteorology including disaster warning, and Indian Remote Sensing (IRS) satellite system for resources survey and management.

INSAT

INSAT system is a joint venture of the Department of Space (DOS), Department of Telecommunications (DOT), India Meteorological Department (IMD), All India Radio (AIR) and Doordarshan. The overall coordination and management of INSAT system rests with Secretary-level INSAT Coordination Committee (ICC).

INSAT was established in 1983 with the commissioning of INSAT-113. INSAT is one of the largest domestic communication satellite systems in the world today with five satellites, three of them, INSAT-2A, INSAT-213 and INSAT-2C, having been built indigenously. INSAT-1D, launched in June, 1990, is the last of the first-generation INSAT satellites procured from the US. It has already completed eight years of operation and is now in an inclined orbit but still being used for meteorological imaging and a few other services.

INSAT-2 series

The first of indigenously built INSAT satellites, INSAT-

2A, was launched by the European Ariane launch vehicle on July 10, 1992. Located at 74 degree east longitude in the geostationary orbit, it is now in an inclined orbit but used for some of the communication services. INSAT-2B was launched on July 23,1993, also by the Ariane launch vehicle. It is located at 93.5 degree east longitude and is still in service.

INSAT-2A and INSAT-213 are identical and carry the following payloads:

- Twelve national coverage telecommunications (Fixed Satellite Service-FSS) transponders of 36 MHz bandwidth each operating in 5930-6425 MHz (earth to satellite) and 3705-4200 MHz (satellite to earth) frequency bands, with 32 dBW (min) End Of Life (EOL) effective isotropic radiated power (eirp) over the primary coverage area.
- Six extended C-band transponders operating in the 4.5-4.8 GHz frequency band (2 transponders of 34 dBW eirp).
- Two high-power national coverage TV broadcast (Broadcast Satellite Service - BSS) transponders operating in 5850-5930 MHz (earth to satellite) and 2550-2630 MHz (satellite to earth) frequency bands, each capable of handling one direct broadcast (community reception) TV channel and seven low level carriers for services like radio programme distribution, disaster warning, etc., with a 42 dBW (min) EOL eirp over the primary coverage area. These transponders also support dissemination of disaster warning and standard time and frequency signals. A Very High Resolution Radiometer (VHRR) for meteorological earth imaging in visible (0.55-

0.75 micrometre) and infrared (10.5-12.5 micrometre) bands, with resolutions of 2 km and 8 km respectively, having half hourly full earth coverage and sectorscan capability.

- A data relay transponder having global receive coverage with a 402.75 MHz earth to satellite link for relay of meteorological, hydrological and oceanographic data from unattended land and ocean-based automatic data collection-cumûtransmission platforms.
- A 406 MHz/C-band search and rescue distress alert transponder.

INSAT-2C

INSAT-2C was launched by an Ariane launch vehicle on December 7, 1995 and was commissioned on February 10, 1996. It is colocated with INSAT-213 at 93.5 degree east longitude. INSAT-2C comprises the following payloads:

C-band fixed satellite services

- Twelve Normal C-band (5.9-6.4 GHz in the uplink and 3.7-4.2 GHz in the downlink) transponders out of which seven channels (1, 2, 3,. 5, 7, 9 and 10) use 10 W SSPAs, providing EOC (Edge of Coverage) eirp of 36 dBW, three channels (4,6 and 8) use 4 W SSPAs to provide EOC eirp of 32 dBW and two channels (11 and 12) use 50 W TWTAs providing EOC eirp of 36 dBW.
- Six extended C-band (6.75-7.00 GHz in the uplink and 4.50-4.75 GHz in the downlink) transponders out of which two channels (13 and 14) use 10 W SSPAs to provide EOC eirp of 35 dBW and four channels (15, 16, 17 and 18) use 4 W SSPAs providing EOC eirp of 32 dBW.
- Channels 11 and 12 are used for providing

expanded area transmit coverage over south east, central and west Asia, while the remaining channels have Indian national coverage.

Ku-band fixed satellite services

- Three Ku-band (14.25-14.50 GHz in the uplink and 11.45-11.70 GHz in the downlink) transponders using 20 W TWTAs, providing an EOC eirp of 41 dBW The coverage beams essentially encompass the four major metro cities of India. This payload also has a beacon transmitter at Ku-band to assist tracking of large size ground terminals.

Broadcast satellite services

- One CxS band (5.91 GHz in the uplink and 2.61 GHz in the downlink) transponder using 50 W S-band TWTA for broadcasting television and radio programmes over the Indian land mass including the offshore islands. The EOC eirp over the Indian main land is 42 dBW

Mobile Satellite Services (MSS)

- Two communication links - forward link between the hub and mobile station operates in CxS band (6.46 GHz in the uplink and 2.51 GHz downlink) and return link between the mobile station and the hub operates in SxC band (2.68 GHz uplink and 3.69 GHz downlink). While 4W SSPA is used for the C-band downlink transmit section (with EOC eirp of 30 dBW), 50 W TWTA is used for the S-band downlink to provide EOC eirp, of 35 dBW The coverage beam for both MSS transmit and receive functions is wide enough to cover from about 5 degree south latitude to 45 degree north latitude.

INSAT-2DT

INSAT-213, identical to INSAT-2C, was launched on June 4, 1997 but the satellite became in-operable since October 4, 1997 following a power bus anomaly and associated problems. In order to partly augment the capacity of the INSAT system consequent to the loss of INSAT-21), an in-orbit satellite, ARABSAT-1C was acquired from ARABSAT which is a regional inter-governmental satellite consortium of Arab States. The satellite, designated as INSAT-213T, is located at 55 degree east.

INSAT-2DT has 25 Normal C-band transponders and, one S-band BSS transponder. The transponders are being used by Doordarshan and Department of Telecommunications.

Leased capacity

Seven high-power C-band transponders have also been leased from THAICOM-3 of the Shinawatra Satellite Public Co., Thailand, for a period of one year from August 1998. This satellite is located at 78.5 degree east longitude.

INSAT-2E

INSAT-2E is slated for launch in early 1999. INSAT-2E will carry the following complement of payloads:

- Seventeen C-band and lower extended C-band 36 dBW transponders with zonal and global coverage. The zonal coverage channels use 32 W TWTAs and global coverage channels use 60 W TWTAs.
- A Very High Resolution Radiometer (VHRR) similar to that on board INSAT-2A/2B but, in addition, has a water vapour channel (5.7-7.1 microns) with 2 km resolution in visible and 8 km resolution in infrared and water vapour channels respectively.

- A Charge Coupled Device (CCD) camera in the visible (0.63-0.69 micron), near infrared (0.770.86 micron) and short-wave infrared (1.55-1.70 micron) bands with 1 km resolution.

Under an agreement with the International Telecommunications Satellite organisation (INTELSAT), eleven 36 MHz equivalent units of C-band capacity on INSAT-2E will be leased to INTELSAT.

INSAT-3

Five satellites, INSAT-3A through INSAT-3E, are planned to be designed and built under INSAT-3 series. The launches of INSAT-3A and INSAT-3B are planned in 1999-2000. Launch of INSAT-3B, which will carry extended C-band transponders, has been advanced to precede that of INSAT-3A in order to meet expeditiously the requirement of extended C-band capacity of INSAT system.

The following payloads are planned to be included in the INSAT-3 series of satellites: INSAT-3E payloads are under finalisation.

Payloads on INSAT-3 Satellites

Payload	*INSAT-3A*	*INSAT-3B*	*INSAT-3C*	*INSAT-3D*
1	2	3	4	5
Normal C-band Transponder	12	–	24	–
Extended C-band Transponder	6	12	6	–
Ku-band Transponder	6	3	–	–
DRT-SAR	1	–	–	1
S-band Transponder	–	–	2	–
S-MSS Transponder	–	1	1	–

(Contd. . .)

Very High Resolution Radiometer	1	–	–	–
CCD Camera	1	–	–	–
Meteorological Sounder	–	–	–	1
Meteorological Imager	–	–	–	1

GSAT

GSATs are planned to be launched using the developmental test flights of India's Geosynchronous Satellite Launch Vehicle (GSLV). GSAT will enable to develop and test cost-effective hardware elements for S-band digital audio, video, data broadcasting systems, and to demonstrate their applications through experimental start-up services. Some of these applications include digital sound broadcasting, Internet services, distance education, developmental communications and compressed digital TV services.

GSAT-1 to be launched on board the first developmental flight of GSLV will have two S-band transponders, one C-band transponder (Africa coverage) and two C-band transponder for Indian coverage. The follow-on GSAT is planned to carry Ka-band transponder.

INSAT Master Control Facility (MCF)

INSAT Master Control Facility (MCF) at Hassan in Karnataka provides telemetry tracking and command services for INSAT series of satellites. MCF carries out initial orbit raising of satellite as well as in-orbit testing of payload. It closely interacts with user agencies for payload operations.

MCF consists of five Satellite Control Earth Stations (SCES). SCES-1 is built around a fully steerable 14m diameter parabolic antenna, a 7.2m and 7.5m diameter limited steerable antennae. SCES-2, similar to SCES-1, has been augmented with two 7.2m diameter antennae. SCES-3, with 11m diameter full motion antenna, is used for multisatellite ranging operations. SCES-4 is built with multiple antennae to support TTC operations, VHRR, DCP, Ext-C and lower Ext-C band frequencies. SCES-5 is for Ku-band operations and consists of 7.2m diameter limited motion antenna. Another earth station (SCES-6) is being added for INSAT-2E and INSAT-3 series of satellites and it will have a full motion antenna with 9.2/1 1m diameter antenna. The Spacecraft Control Centre (SCC) of MCF is equipped with satellite health monitoring and control equipment, uplink and downlink baseband chains, computing systems, recording systems, payload checkout systems and data links.

INSAT services

Telecommunications

A total of 382 telecommunication terminals of various sizes and capabilities (excluding NICNET, RABMN and VSAT microterminals) are operating in INSAT telecommunications network providing 5,750 two-way speech circuits or equivalent over 166 routes. These include 124 fixed and captive, 20 transportable, 14 VVIP/Special terminals, 20 fly-away terminals and 174 Multi-Channels Per Carrier Very Small Aperture Terminals (MCPC VSATs and 15 Pvt. VSAT hubs). Over 400 additional earth stations are under various stages of implementation in the DOT network. In the National Informatics Centre Network (NICNET), there are over 800 microterminals. Twelve closed user group 64 kbps data networks are currently operating through INSAT extended C-band transponders. About 600 VSATs are operating under the Remote Area Business Management Network. Under Remote Rural Area Communications using MCPC VSATs, 174 VSATs are operational in the

DOT network. Another 150 VSATs are being added. High speed VSAT Network (HVNET) terminals are being offered on lease for data-only terminal and for data and voice service. Seventeen long distance subscriber telephone terminals are operational and 20 more are under consideration. The planned Bangalore-Delhi digital network with two 34 Mbps streams being commissioned shortly. Augmentation of existing 8 Mbps connectivities amongst four metros is planned by using digital channel multiplying equipment.

Captive satellite-based networks for National Thermal Power Corporation (NTPC), Gas Authority of India Ltd (GAIL), Nuclear Power Corporation (NPC), Indian Telephone Industries (ITI), Oil and Natural Gas Commission (ONGC), National Fertilisers Limited (NFL) and Coal India Limited (CIL) are operational. A CIL earth station at Poonch has been commissioned. The National Stock Exchange (NSE) VSAT network in extended C-band is operational. A number of captive government networks are also working with INSAT More organisations are in the process of implementing their own captive networks using INSAT capacity. DOT has licensed a few private operators to provide value-added services to the public using the extended C-band.

Mobile satellite services

With the launch of INSAT-2C in December 1995, an S-band Mobile Satellite Service (MSS) has been added to the INSAT system. The following three classes of services were identified for MSS:

- Class A: low bit rate encoded voice, data and fax services using demand assigned SCPC channels, with mobile and portable (suit-case size) terminals. Five terminals have been installed as pre-operational service.

- Class B: low bit rate store-and-forward messaging service using shared channels with mobile and portable terminals.
- Class C: low bit rate reporting service using shared channels with portable and hand-held terminals. The INSAT-MSS is targeted at land mobile and maritime users. The MSS hub located at Bangalore has been tested with the INSAT-2C MSS transponders.

INSAT system is at present used to provide a unique one-way messaging to user headquarters using a small hand-held terminal using INSAT-MSS transponder. The Delhi Earth Station (DES) of DOS is used as the hub in this experimental service. Short messages from user terminals are relayed through the satellite to the hub and are automatically forwarded to the respective user headquarters via Fax or data links. This reporting service is provided using small hand-held terminal weighing only about a kilogram. The network manager at the hub keeps track of the destination addresses for the mobile user messages and -forwards it through fax or data interfaces.

INSAT-3B satellite planned for launch in 1999-2000 will carry an S-band MSS payload similar to the one carried by INSAT-2C. INSAT type-A and C band MSS services are expected to become operational with the commissioning of INSAT-3B.

Television

INSAT has been a major catalyst for the rapid expansion of television coverage in India. Satellite television now covers over 65 percent of the Indian land mass and over 80 percent of the Indian population. Four S-band transponders, ten C-band transponders and four extended C-band transponders on board INSAT-2A, 2B, 2C and INSAT-11) are providing the following satellite television services:

- National networking service (DD-1), North-Eastern States and Assam regional service in 2.5 GHz band on CxS transponder of INSAT-11) and INSAT-2B.
- Regional services in 3.7-4.2 GHz band and 4.2-4.5 GHz extended C-band transponders of INSAT-213, INSAT-2C and INSAT-2DT; Kerala, Karnataka and Jammu & Kashmir, Tamil Nadu, West Bengal, Andhra Pradesh, National, Metro television, Maharashtra, Punjab, Himachal Pradesh, Jammu & Kashmir regional services are supported by these satellites.

Doordarshan's national service is being supported on CxS transponder of INSAT-11). Doordarshan programmes are sent to DOT earth station at Sikanderabad in Bulandshahar district of Uttar Pradesh using terrestrial microwave link from where they are uplinked to the satellite and received by various Doordarshan Centres using Television Receive Only (TVRO) facility and relayed by the transmitters. At present, 1023 transmitters are working in the INSAT system out of which 967 transmitters (83 HPTs, 652 LPTs, 214 VLPTs) and 18 transposers are working in the DD-1 network and 53 TV Transmitters (8 HPTs, 42 LPTs and 3 VLPTs) are working in the DD-2 network. The DD-3 network has 3 LPTs.

Under INSAT scheme, 2,000 S-band Direct Reception Sets (DRS) have been deployed in Andhra Pradesh, Orissa, Bihar, Uttar Pradesh, Maharashtra and Gujarat. In addition, 2,000, VHF Community TV sets have been deployed in selected villages of Uttar Pradesh, Maharashtra, Bihar and Gujarat. In selected villages of North-Eastern States, 3,820 VHF sets and 365 DRSs have been installed. One hundred VHF community viewing sets have been installed in Sikkim. 650 monochrome sets are proposed to be replaced in Jammu & Kashmir with colour TV sets under a community viewing scheme. Additionally, 550 sets are being installed in this State.

Educational TV

Educational TV (ETV) has been one of the high priority areas for Doordarshan. Curriculum-based programmes are produced with active involvement of State educational administrators and teachers which are telecast from Delhi, Mumbai and Chennai. Satellite based enrichment programmes for school children are produced by the following State Institutes of Educational Technology (SIET) in Marathi at Pune, Gujarati at Ahmedabad, Oriya at Bhubaneshwar and Telugu at Hyderabad which are relayed by all transmitters in the concerned States. Hindi programmes are produced at State Institutes of Educational Technology at Delhi, Lucknow and Patna which are relayed by all transmitters in Uttar Pradesh, Rajasthan, Bihar, Madhya Pradesh, Haryana, Himachal Pradesh and Delhi.

Programmes for University students are produced by Education Media Research Centres and Audio Visual Research Centres at different places. These enrichment programmes provide quality education within the reach of students in small towns and villages. Syllabus-based programmes for students enrolled in Indira Gandhi National Open University (IGNOU) are telecast on the national network as follows:

Daily	0600-0700
Monday - Friday	0715-0800
Monday-Friday	1000-1030
Monday - Friday	1100-1200

The programmes are telecast on DD-2 between 12 midnight and 12.30 a.m. from Monday to Friday. Educational Television/School Television programmes are telecast from Regional Kendras between 10.30 and 11.00 a.m. from Monday to Friday.

Satellite-Based Training and Developmental Communications Channel (TDCC)

Training and Developmental Communication Channel (TDCC) using INSAT which is operational since 1995, provides a unique one-way video and two-way audio system of interactive education where teaching-end includes a simple studio and uplink terminal for transmitting live or pre-recorded lectures. The participants at the class-rooms located nation-wide receive lectures through simple dish antennas and have facility to interact with lectures using telephone lines. The TDCC system is being used extensively by several agencies and industries like Indira Gandhi National Open University, National Dairy Development Board, State Bank of India and several State Governments (Gujarat, Karnataka and Madhya Pradesh) for distance education in rural development, women and child development, Panchayati Raj and industrial training. At present, there are about 375 receive terminals set up by various user agencies which is expected to grow to about 2,000 in the near future.

New digital interactive techniques in TDCC is planned to improve the capacity and quality of the system. It will also enable off-line downloading of lessons from servers at teaching end by the students.

Jhabua Development Communications Project (JDCP)

JDCP which was started on November 1, 1996, is aimed at setting up an operational satellite-based broadcast and interactive network for developmental communication and training. Under JDCP, 150 Direct Reception Systems DRSs) and 12 talk-back terminals have been installed in Jhabua district of Madhya Pradesh. JDCP is now fully operational. Inter-active training programmes are conducted during the day. Evening transmissions are addressed to the rural audience. More than 1,200 programmers have been produced by ISRO and private producers during the two years of operation. The impact of JDCP has been evaluated and it is found that there is a significant gain in knowledge and information among the viewers.

It has been decided to expand the project to cover an additional 462 sites in Jhabua. In addition, 200 DRS terminals will be added in adjacent districts of Dhar and Barwani. JDCP network will also be upgraded to digital broadcast technology. DOS has proposed to hand-over operation of JDCP to Madhya Pradesh Government.

Radio networking

Radio Networking (RN) through INSAT provides a reliable high-fidelity 10/15 kHz programme channels for national as well as regional networking. At present, 195 All India Radio (AIR) stations have been equipped with S-band receive terminals and 17 with C-band terminals. RN of INSAT system primarily uses CxS band transponder in Single Channel Per Carrier mode. The RN carriers are injected at a low level into the high power CxS band transponders along with the TV carrier. The programmes received on these S-band receive terminals are rebroadcast by terrestrial transmitters. Interactive exchange of programmes also takes place between any two or more uplink stations .

There are 32 RN channels at present operating in S-band and 7 in C-band. Single channel captive uplink earth stations at 13 major programme producing centres (Srinagar, Ahmedabad, Bhopal, Cuttack, Patna, Guwahati, Shillong Thiruvananthapuram, Hyderabad, Bangalore, Jaipur, Shimla and Lucknow) have been provided. These are: the captive earth station at Broadcasting House (BH), Mumbai, provides uplink of two Vividh Bharati channels. The earth station at BH, Delhi, has been augmented to provide uplink for 7 RN carriers in CxS band. 23 RN carriers are operating in INSAT-2C and 9 RN carriers in INSAT-2B S-1 and S-2. Seven RN channels are uplinked from BH, Delhi to operate with CxC transponder of INSAT-2B. These programmes are being received by 16 major AIR stations (Mumbai, Guwahati, Hyderabad, Rajkot, Chennai, Bangalore SPT, Bangalore, Aligarh, Gorakhpur, Dharwad, Alleppey, Cuttack, Chinsurah, Nagpur, Ahmedabad and Bhopal). Another 20 stations are planned to be added to the network.

Four transportable uplink terminals have been acquired by AIR for coverage of events taking place at remote locations and for relay of programmes directly from the spot via INSAT AIR has also acquired a DSNG RN terminal which is capable of uplinking CD quality music channel from any remote locations to a central place such as Delhi.

S-Band data broadcast experiments using GSAT-1

GSAT-1, to be launched using developmental test flights of GSLV will carry S-band broadcast payload. A set of applications using digital broadcast technology have been identified under GSAT application programme. Digital Sound and Data Broadcasting (DSDB) will provide simultaneous transmission of CD quality music and low bit rate data transmission to small portable terminals. Data transmission capability of DSDB system can be utilised for transmission of news, pictures and multi-media contents to distant locations. DSDB system also provides a reliable solution f or disaster warning. IMD is exploring the possibility of using DSDB receivers for cyclone warning.

It is planned to utilise S-band data broadcast channels to deliver Internet data at high speed to remote locations. It is also planned to set up a hybrid satellite-terrestrial network for high speed Internet access using S-band data broadcast. S-band channels will also be utilised to deliver digital TV using Digital Video Broadcast (DVB) standard.

Satellite news gathering and dissemination

Satellite News Gathering using INSAT system enables on the spot real-time news coverages. Prasar Bharati is procuring five Outdoor Broadcast (OB) SNG terminals to cover important events in different locations for transmission via satellite to a central station at Delhi for rebroadcast over DD channels.

Press Trust of India (PTI) is implementing a system to provide its news and information services at higher speed and increased volume and variety directly to a wider range of media and other users by utilising the broadcast facilities of INSAT-ID satellite. The project utilises a Radio Networking (RN) type of channel on one of the broadcast (CxS) transponders of the satellite. The PTI satellite news and facsimile dissemination project is working with 15 terminals (14 from PTI and one shared with AIR).

Meteorology

The meteorological data of INSAT is processed and disseminated by the INSAT Meteorological Data Processing System (IMDPS) of India Meteorological Department (IMD). Upper winds, sea surface temperature and precipitation index data are regularly obtained. The 0600 hour GMT (Greenwich Mean Time), VHRR image-derived wind data are provided on Global Telecommunications System (GTS) of the World Meteorological Organisation (WMO -The 0300 hours GMT full disc infrared pictures are transmitted as radio facsimile broadcast daily for reception in the neighbouring countries.

INSAT-VHRR imageries are used by Doordarshan during news coverage and by newspapers as part of weather reporting. At present, repetitive and synoptic weather system observations over Indian Ocean from geostationary orbit are available only from INSAT system. INSAT VHRR data is available in near real-time at 27 Meteorological Data Dissemination Centres (MDDC) in various parts of the country. With the commissioning of direct satellite service for processed VHRR data, MDDC type of data can be provided at any location in the country.

One hundred meteorological Data Collection Platforms (DCPs) have been installed all over the country and also at Schiramacher, the Indian base station in Antarctica. The DCP services are provided using the Data Relay Transponders of INSAT-2B. Use of the INSAT DRT is also being contemplated by Narmada Control Authority (NCA) and Central Water Commission (CWC) for real-time hydrometeorological data collection in the Narmada, Mahanadi and Chambal basins. CWC is planning to commission 40 DCP terminals in Narmada basin during 1999-2000.

About 250 Cyclone Warning Dissemination System (CWDS) receivers have been installed in the selected cyclone-prone coastal areas of Andhra Pradesh, north Tamil Nadu, Orissa, West Bengal and Gujarat, with DWS uplink from Chennai, Mumbai and Calcutta. The receivers are selectively addressable. IMD is upgrading its system at New Delhi for processing the meteorological data from INSAT-2E to be launched shortly. The INSAT-2E will carry a 3-channel VHRR including a water vapour channel and a 3-channel CCD camera.

Satellite Aided Search and Rescue (SAS&R)

As a Member of the International COSPAS-SARSAT

programme for providing distress alert and position location service through LEOSAR (Low Earth Orbit Search and Rescue) satellite system, India has established two Local User Terminals (LUTs) - one at Lucknow and the other at Bangalore. The Indian Mission Control Centre (INMCC) is colocated at Bangalore.

In addition, INSAT-2A and INSAT-2B are equipped with 406 MHz Search and Rescue transponders, which pick up and relay alert signals originating from the distress beacons of maritime, aviation and land users. During the year, INSAT, along with the GOES satellite of USA, provided globally, Demonstration and Evaluation (D&E) data and the initial phase operational performance inputs for establishing Geostationary Satellite based Search And Rescue (GEOSAR) systems. The D&E results have proved the merits of GEOSAR system for potential time advantage in distress alert detection and ability for continuous monitoring of alerts over a large coverage area compared to LEOSAR system. Based on the performance demonstrations of INSAT and GOES, these two systems have been now adopted as an integral part of the International COSPAS-SARSAT system for satellite aided search and rescue operations and they complement the LEOSAR system.

Indian LUTs provide coverage to a large part of Indian Ocean region rendering distress alert services to Bangladesh, Bhutan, Kenya, Maldives, Nepal, Seychelles, Somalia, Sri Lanka and Tanzania. The operations of INMCC/LUT are funded by the participating agencies, namely, Coast Guard, Airports Authority of India (AAI) and Director General of Shipping and Services.

INSAT GEOSAR Local User Terminal (GEO LUT) is also established at ISTRAC, Bangalore and integrated with INMCC. The distress alert messages concerning the Indian service area, detected at INMCC are passed on to

Indian Coast Guard and Rescue Coordination Centres (RCCs) at Mumbai, Calcutta, Delhi and Chennai. The search and rescue activities are carried out by Coast Guard, Navy and Air Force. The INMCC is linked to the RCCs and other International MCCs through automatic telex and Aeronautical Fixed Telecommunication Network (AFTN). The Indian LUTs and MCC provide service round-the-clock and maintains the data base of all 406 Mhz registered beacons equipped on Indian ships and aircraft.

The Indian LUTs and INMCCs have been upgraded during the year to detect new location protocols from Geographical Position System integrated beacons and also to be compatible with data formats of new satellites of COSPAS-SARSAT system.

The distress events supported by INMCC during the year include the following incidents:

- On July 21, 1998 INMCC picked up a 406 MHz distress signal from Belieze registered vessel MV Osool which sank in Arabian Sea because of bad weather. INMCC transmitted message to RCC and Coast Guard of Mumbai who coordinated the rescue operations and 20 crew members were rescued by near by ship MV Pratibha Godavari.
- A 12 member trekking expedition team activated its distress beacon on August 1, 1998 from the Himalayan range when one of their team members suffered high altitude sickness. The distress alert signal detected by INSAT LUT was transmitted to RCC Delhi which rescued her and took her to a hospital in Manali by an Indian Airforce plane.

Standard time and frequency signal dissemination services

A Standard Time and Frequency Signal Dissemination Service (STFSDS), using a radio networking (RN) type CxS carrier on, INSAT-1D, is being operated by the National Physical Laboratory (NPL). This service is available round-the-clock in a broadcast mode at downlink frequency in S-band and is receivable on a set-up consisting of a 2.4 m diameter antenna, a front-end converter, an FM demodulator and a microprocessor controlled signal decoder. The STFSDS consists of a train of 5 kHz bursts which is frequency modulated on the carrier.

The time has a precision of better than one microsecond and accuracy of better than 20 microsecond.

Satellite navigation

It is expected that in the next five years, many advanced countries like United States, Japan, Europe, New Zealand, Australia and Canada will have satellite navigation service. The International Civil Aviation Organisation has made Satellite navigation equipment mandatory on all civilian aircraft. To upgrade the existing Communications Navigation and Surveillance (CNS) and Air-Traffic Management (ATM) system in India, Airports Authority of India (AAI) is planning to make them adaptable to Future Air Navigation System (FANS) through the introduction of Indian Wide Area Differential GPS (WADGPS) system. Department of Space plans to play a vital role in establishing the satellite navigation infrastructure. Several studies related to signal generation and uplink from Navigation Land Earth Station (NLES) in India to GSO Nav payload, establishment of monitoring stations, inter-linking of national and international monitoring stations, necessary measurement campaigns, system development and testing and introduction of GSO Navigation payloads in Indian and other satellites and establishment of Mission Control Centre for satellite based navigation have been undertaken.

Frequency management

Implementation of space programme involves access to orbit spectrum resources. The selection of S-band for Indian satellite and launch vehicle TTC network, coordination of three orbital slots for the first and second generation INSAT satellite networks, coordination of new frequency bands in C-band and Ku-band and wider coverages for regional satellite network operations under INSAT coordination of frequencies for INSAT-VSAT operations in user premises, coordination of frequencies for scientific radars have been the highlights of Frequency Management activities. The orbit-frequency coordination work carried out to make available the fourth orbital slot at 55 degree east for positioning and operating INSAT-2131 Bilateral coordination meetings have been held with Russia, INTELSAT and Japan and notifications were prepared and sent to the International Telecommunications Union (ITU), for orbit-frequency coordination of INSAT-2E satellite systems, scheduled for launch in 1999 for lease of transponders to INTELSAT

Frequency management also involves participation in the work of International Telecommunications Union (ITU) conferences and meetings to protect national interests in frequency allocations and related subjects. DOS has also undertaken the responsibility of convening National Working Group on space matters as a part of national preparatory committee work for World Radio Conferences. DOS also continues to participate in Space Frequency Coordination Group (SFCG) which is an informal forum for all space agencies to discuss frequency coordination issues for space science services.

Follow-up actions have been taken for orbit-frequency coordination of future INSAT systems for providing Direct-to-Home (DTH) and broad-band communications services in Ka-band. For INSAT-3 series of satellites, actions for additional coordination have been initiated and necessary filings made with ITU. In the remote sensing area, coordination of forthcoming IRS-P4 and IRS-P5 have been taken up.

National Natural Resources Management System (NNRMS)

National Natural Resources Management System (NNRMS), for which DOS is the nodal agency, is aimed at optimal management of country's natural resources using space-based remote sensing in conjunction with conventional techniques. NNRMS activities are coordinated at the national level by the Planning Committee of NNRMS (PC-NNRMS) which provides guidelines for implementation of the system and also oversees the progress of remote sensing applications for natural resources management. The NNRMS activities are reviewed and guided by nine Standing Committees - (i) Agriculture & Soils, (ii) Bio-Resources, (iii) Geology and Mineral Resources, (iv) Water Resources, (v) Ocean Resources, (vi) Cartography & Mapping, (vii) Urban Management, (viii) Rural Development and (ix) Technology and Training.

The major elements of NNRMS encompass conceptualisation and implementing the space systems with associated ground-based data reception, processing and interpretation systems and integrating satellite-based data with conventional data for resource management.

Space segment

Indian Remote Sensing (IRS) satellite system commissioned with the launch of IRS-1A, in March 1988 is the mainstay of NNRMS. IRS system comprises of four satellites, IRS-113, launched in August 1991. IRS-1C launched in December 1995, IRS-P3 launched in March

1996 and IRS-113, launched in August 1996. IRS-1C and IRS-113 which carry a unique combination of camera payloads, are the world's best civilian remote sensing satellites in orbit. IRS-P4 (OCEANSAT) is planned for launch on board PSLV-C2 in 1999-2000. It will carry an Ocean Colour Monitor (OCM), a Multi-frequency Scanning Microwave Radiometer (MSMR), both of which will be used for oceanographic applications. IRS-P5 (CARTOSAT), planned to be launched by PSLV in 2000-01 is designed for mapping applications. It will carry two Panchromatic cameras with 2.5 m resolution and a swath of 30 km. These cameras will provide stereo images for generating Digital Terrain Models (DTM)/Digital Elevation Models (DEM).

IRS-P6 (RESOURCESAT) planned for launch in 2001-02 will be similar to IRS-IC and IRS-1D but with several improvements. It will have multispectral camera LISS-III with 23.6 metre spatial resolution in all four bands and another high resolution multispectral camera, LISS-IV providing better than 6 metre resolution ' The Advanced Wide Field Sensor (AWiFS) camera of IRS-P6 will have a spatial resolution of around 70 metre in three bands and a swath of 400 km.

The ISRO Telemetry, Tracking and Command Network (ISTRAC), with its Spacecraft Control Centre (SCC) at Bangalore and TTC Stations located at Bangalore, Lucknow, Mauritius and Bearslake, provides mission support to IRS satellites.

Data reception, processing and dissemination

Remote sensing data reception from IRS-IB, IRS-1C, IRS-1D and IRS-P3, as well as from USAs LANDSAT-5, NOAA-12 and 14 and Europe's ERS-1 and ERS-2 is being carried out by NRSA Data Reception Station at Shadnagar. NRSA Data Centre (NDC) disseminates IRS data products. Standard, customised and non-standard services are provided to about 1700 users. The average turn-around-time for the data supply is less than ten days. About 12,500 data products of various satellites have been supplied to users during the year till December 1998. Data acquisition and data processing systems are being further augmented by high-performance, high-throughput workstations.

Aerial remote sensing

Aerial remote sensing is carried out for specific mappings application like urban planning, infrastructure planning and aeromagnetic surveys. A total of 383 hours of flying was undertaken during the year. Preparation of large scale base maps for infrastructure planning has been taken up for Hyderabad Water Supply and Sewerage Board and Bangalore Water Supply and Sewerage Board and Bangalore Development Authority. Large scale mapping of 25 towns for Town and Country Planning Organisation (TCPO) has been completed and another 11 towns have been taken up for mapping.

Remote sensing applications

Remote sensing data is used for several resources survey and management applications. Application projects of national relevance are carried out with the involvement of user agencies both at central and state levels. The progress made in the application of space-based remote sensing is highlighted in the following paragraphs.

Agriculture and soils

Pre-harvest Crop Acreage and Production Estimation (CAPE) of major crops using remote sensing data is one of the major application projects being carried out in collaboration with state and central agencies. CAPE covers six major crops, namely, rice, wheat, sorghum, cotton, mustard and groundnut in 15 states (Andhra Pradesh, Assam, Bihar, Gujarat, Haryana, Himachal Pradesh, Karnataka, Orissa, Maharashtra, Madhya

Pradesh, Punjab, Rajasthan, Tamil Nadu, Uttar Pradesh and West Bengal). The forecast includes district-level production.

A project on Forecasting Agricultural output using Space, Agrometeorology and Land observation (FASAL) has been initiated. FASAL has been implemented on a pilot scale in Orissa during Kharif 1998-99 for rice with the participation of Orissa Remote Sensing Applications Centre (ORSAC), and other concerned departments and Orissa University of Agriculture and Technology. Three forecasts of Kharif rice have been made - rice area and yield using meteorological models and district-wise rice area using microwave remote sensing data and yield using meteorological models.

Under National Wheat Production Forecasting, in-season forecasts for wheat were generated using multi-date WiFS data of IRS. Rabi cropped area for wheat growing districts in six states (Bihar, Uttar Pradesh, Madhya Pradesh, Punjab, Haryana and Rajasthan) was estimated.

Agro-climatic Planning and Information Bank (APIB) is being established on a pilot scale at Regional Remote Sensing Service Centre, Bangalore at the instance of Planning Commission. APIB will provide single window access for information related to agriculture and allied sectors. Data-base for seeds, package of practices, fertilisers, plant protection chemicals, farm machinery, etc., has already been created during the year. Weekly rainfall probabilities and crop growing periods have been identified for all taluks in Tumkur district of Karnataka and spatial resources data generated for Bijapur, Tumkur and Shimoga districts. Cadastral level land use/land cover maps have also been generated in a few villages to demonstrate feasibility of providing information on survey number-wise.

Under National Agricultural Drought Assessment and Management System (NADAMS) crop and seasonal conditions assessment report for 11 states (Andhra Pradesh, Bihar, Gujarat, Haryana, Karnataka, Maharashtra, Madhya Pradesh, Orissa, Rajasthan, Tamil Nadu and Uttar Pradesh) at district level has been prepared for 1998 Kharif season June to October) and sent to the concerned agencies of the respective states and also to Ministry of Agriculture, New Delhi. It is proposed to enlarge the scope of NADAMS during Ninth Five Year Plan by using high resolution IRS data.

Farm level sugarcane mapping for Krishna valley project under lift irrigation scheme has been completed. Sugarcane acreage estimation for ten command areas of sugar mills in Haryana was completed during the year.

Impact assessment of sodic land reclamation project in Uttar Pradesh has been carried out using data from IRS LISS-III and PAN camera on a pilot scale and it has provided an accuracy of 95 percent in the assessment. A project on banana orchards acreage estimation for Tiruchirapalli in Tamil Nadu has also been completed and an accuracy in acreage estimation is found to be better than 90 percent. Classification of soils in part of Puri district of Orissa, using elevation, slope and lithology of the area, has been carried out and an improvement of 5.5 percent achieved in classification accuracy.

Forestry and ecology

At the behest of Department of Biotechnology, a project to prioritise biologically rich areas in North-Eastern region, Western Ghats and Western Himalayas has been taken up. The project envisages characterising biodiversity at landscape level using remote sensing data and geographic information system on various ecological parameters like forest fragmentation, porosity, patchiness, juxtaposition, interspersion, etc. Prospecting of these regions will be based on the sum of all these parameters. In Phase-I of the project, vegetation mapping in digital form will be prepared on 1:250,000 scale using IRS data. The methodology has already been developed based on pilot studies in Meghalaya and Madhya Pradesh.

Under Forest Resources Assessment in Madhya Pradesh, a pilot study has been initiated to bring out maps to help in scientific management of forests using remote sensing data. Stock map, infrastructure maps, drainage/watershed map and s lope map have been prepared and block-level timber volume estimation carried out based on ground inventory. The growing stock map has been generated using IRS-PAN data. Under Forest Biomass Estimation Project, a methodology has been developed to estimate tree volume from satellite data using direct and indirect approaches in Sal plantations of Gorakhpur Forest division. Similar study is also being carried out in natural moist deciduous forest in Uttar Pradesh.

Occurrence of fire in Gir Forest in Gujarat has been monitored using IRS-1C, and IRS-1D, and data and the spatial information provided to Gujarat Forest Department.

As part of IGBP biodiversity study is being carried out for Central Himalaya to quantify biodiversity, to examine relationship between biodiversity and bio-physical/environmental variables and to find the effects of diversity on ecosystem functioning. The study indicates that three prominent altitudinal zones in the area are expected to have maximum impact of global climatic change. The second phase of the study covering entire Indian Central Himalaya has been initiated. A study covering Garhwal in Himalaya, mapping of forest biomass and quantification of fuel and fodder availability has been undertaken.

Elephant corridor mapping has been carried out covering entire North Bengal using IRS LISS-III data. Details on vegetation cover, soil, slope, availability of food and water have been mapped which are used to develop habitat suitability map. Three major elephant routes have been identified in addition to five other corridors along the international border.

A study has been carried out for identifying changes between pre-establishment and postûestablishment phases of Kudremukh Iron Ore Company Limited (KIOCL) in Western Ghats of Karnataka. Multi-temporal satellite data have been used, with special reference to mine development and different reclamation activities, including evaluation of biomass, species composition, growing stock and land cover changes.

Geology

A project on Resources Data base Generation and Landslide Hazard Zonation in Mizoram State has been taken up to generate a digital data base of the natural resources on 1:250,000 scale. Various resource maps such as land use/land cover, lithology and structure, geomorphology, slope, drainage and watershed and soil have been prepared using IRS LISS-II and collateral data for the entire state.

Study of landslides in Uttar Pradesh has been taken up using IRS-1C/1D PAN and LISS-II data on geology, geomorphology and other terrain characteristics based on which the areas prone for landslides can be identified.

An inter-agency pilot project on Geological Information System for Maharashtra and Madhya Pradesh has been taken up to create a data base for mineral prospecting and environmental studies. Sites for lignite exploration in Kutchch area have been explored using IRS data. An integrated study of aeromagnetic and satellite data has also been carried out over Kutchch basin to identify suitable structural anomalies for hydrocarbon exploration. Environmental impact due to coal mining in Raniganj coal belt area of Burdwan district, West Bengal has been carried out and alternative measures recommended to reduce the impact.

Land use/land cover

The final phase of Wastelands Mapping covering 192 districts of India has been taken up for Department of Wastelands Development, Ministry of Rural Areas and Employment. Generation of wasteland data base in digital form is carried out using both digital analysis and visual interpretation of IRS LISS-III data. Land use/Land cover assessment of the 10 km radius zone around the proposed power plant in Hirakund, Orissa, has been carried out for the Indian Aluminum Company. Land degradation and land use studies of Som-Amba-Kamla command area in Rajasthan has been conducted using two season (Rabi and Kharif) IRS LISS-III data for Institute of Development Studies, Jaipur. Land use mapping around Gujarat Ambhuja Cements Ltd. near Kodinar, Gujarat has been carried out using temporal IRS LISS-II data. Other ancillary information related to forest boundaries, mining lease areas, etc., has also been provided to the users.

Urban land use planning and development

Preparation of development plan of Pimpri-Chinchwad Municipal Corporation upto the year 2018 has been taken up. A spatial framework of the area has been created in Geographical Information System environment and IRS LISS-III and Panchromatic data products generated. Development plan for Ahmedabad Urban Development Authority (AUDA) has been carried out using IRS-1C PAN + LISS-III merged data.

Ocean studies

Remote sensing has been used for marine applications

under the Marine Remote Sensing Information Services (MARSIS) programme of Department of Ocean Development (DOD). US NOAA satellite data is used for retrieval of Sea Surface Temperatures (SST). Potential zones for fishing is forecast based on SST and the information disseminated to fishermen. The SST are also used for developing data-bases to study oceanography, weather and climate.

Plans for application of data to be received from IRS-P4 Ocean Colour Monitor have been prepared in consultation with participating agencies.

A study on sediment movement under tidal influence has been taken up using multi-temporal WiFS data of IRS-1C/D for Hooghly estuary and Dhamra estuary (Orissa). An a as on Coasta Land use showing spatial extent of wetland features such as mudflats, beaches, mangroves and land use features such as agricultural land, barren land, forests, etc., has been prepared for the Tamil Nadu, Andaman and Nicobar Islands, Andhra Pradesh, Orissa and West Bengal.

Water resources

A pilot study on ground water draft estimation using satellite data has been taken up for Anantpur district in Andhra Pradesh.

Analysis of the performance of 14 selected command areas across the country has been taken up for Ministry of Water Resources. Of these, 9 command areas Damodar, Mayurakshi and Kangsabati of West Bengal, Chambal of Rajasthan, Jayakwadi, Upper Tapi and Purna of Maharashtra and Jamuna and Shukla of Assam State have been selected in the first phase of the study. Satellite derived information on cropping pattern and crop yield will be used for evaluating the irrigation system performance. Monitoring of command areas has also been taken up in three major command areas, namely, Mahi, Ukai-Kakrapar and Shetrunji under the Centrally sponsored Command Area Development Programme in Gujarat. Watershed prioritisation for 36 blocks for the Government of West Bengal has been taken up and work has completed for 22 blocks. One of these watershed, Kansabati, has also been selected for modelling run-off sediments.

Erosion of river banks at Kaziranga National Park in Assam has been monitored using multi date satellite data and sites identified for preventing erosion. Flood monitoring is continuing with the participation of concerned State governments. During the year flood that occurred in Brahmaputra basin has been monitored and mapped. Floods in Ganga basin has also been monitored. District-wise statistics on the areas affected have been generated for Assam and provided to the Relief Commissioners, Department of Agriculture and Co-operation. (A study has also been made of the Gujarat cyclone during the year).

Forecast of cumulative snow-melt run-off from Sutlej river basin at Bhakra reservoir during April-June is being carried out for the last five years. The forecast, issued in April every year, is used by Bhakra-Beas Management Board for control and scheduling of the Bhakra water for power generation, irrigation, etc. The forecast is accurate to one percent of actual observed inflows into Bhakra reservoir.

Erosion of catchment areas of Chamera-I and II project in Himachal Pradesh have been studied and sensitive areas identified for desilting.

State-wise atlas showing the wetland area in the country has been prepared and the extent of area under wet lands estimated. Detailed studies of 21 notified wetlands have also been made using temporal satellite data.

Grassland mapping

Grassland mapping project in the states of Gujarat, Himachal Pradesh and Tamil Nadu has been taken up for Ministry of Environment and Forest (MOE&F). Classification for the mapping has been finalised and base maps pertaining to each district prepared.

Archaeology

Analysis of IRS LISS-III data in conjunction with collateral information has indicated an unexplored archaeological site near Junagadh. Field study has indicated presence of pottery, bones, stone walls and trench at this site. In another study aimed at locating the course of Saraswati River, satellite data has been used to trace its path from Manasarovar in Tibet to Saurashtra coast in Gujarat.

Integrated mission for sustainable development

Integrated Mission for Sustainable Development (IMSD) was initiated in 1992 to generate localeûspecific action plans for sustainable development of natural resources. Locale-specific prescription are generated under IMSD using data from IRS satellites and collateral socio-economic data. State Remote Sensing Applications Centre, Universities, private entrepreneurs and non-governmental organisations are actively participating in IMSD. Action plans generated for development of watersheds include surface water harvesting through percolation tanks, check dams, farm ponds, vegetation bundling and adoption of sprinkler/drip irrigation systems. Optimum land use and farming systems like fodder and fuel wood plantations, agro forestry, horticulture, improved agricultural technology and aforestation are recommended based on the study of each watershed.

Out of the 175 districts which are included under IMSD, studies have been completed in 24 districts, one priority block each from 80 districts (taken up on specific request from Ministry of Rural Areas and Employment) and 54 watersheds/blocks/areas in the remaining. Implementation of action plans like construction of check dams, nala bunds, recharge wells, gully plugging and deepening of existing tanks is in progress.

Forty-three specific areas from as many districts in 12 states have been specifically selected as models for focussed efforts to ensure utilisation of IMSD inputs for planning as well as strengthening the scientific robustness of action plans. Strategies and frame-work for institutionalisation of IMSD are being discussed with State Governments.

National (Natural) Resources Information System (NRIS)

Significant progress has been made during the year in creating digital data base of natural resources And corresponding attributes data of 18 out of 30 districts in the country selected under NRIS. Data bases for Bijapur in Karnataka, Chandrapur in Maharashtra and Bharathpur in Rajasthan have been established. A comprehensive district development plan is being generated jointly with the district administration and state centres using these data bases. On the software front, two query shells packages have been developed for providing user friendly interaction.

Microwave remote sensing

Microwave data received from satellites like European Remote Sensing Satellite, ERS, has been used for rice crop acreage estimation and condition monitoring and for identification of potato and rice crops on an experimental basis. Discrimination of rice and potato crops in Gangetic plains of West Bengal has been made. A classification accuracy of 94 percent for rice has been obtained. The estimate of crop area could be made within 20 to 30 days of transplantation in the case of rice.

Regional Remote Sensing Service Centres- (RRSSCs)

Regional Remote Sensing Service Centres (RRSSCs) of DOS, located at Bangalore, Dehradun, Jodhpur, Kharagpur and Nagpur continued to carry out various application projects and development of software for carrying out digital analysis-based remote sensing studies and GIS-based studies. RRSSCs completed several projects in the areas of ground water, forest, geology, land use/land cover, fisheries and environmental impacts in collaboration with state and central government agencies. Value-added products were provided for large scale urban/ infrastructure applications. Digital image processing and Geographical Information System (GIS) facilities are being used for national level projects apart from other uses. Agro-climatic Planning and Information Bank (APIB) is being established at Regional Remote Sensing Service Centre, Bangalore at the instance of Planning Commission in order to provide a single window access for information related to agriculture and allied sectors. Training programmes in digital analysis of remote sensing data and GIS also have been conducted to benefit working level scientists during the year.

State remote sensing centres

As the nodal agency of NNRMS, DOS is making efforts for establishing and strengthening State Remote Sensing Applications Centres (SRSAC). At present 23 states have already established SRSACs which are equipped with visual interpretation and digital image processing systems with Geographical Information System (GIS) packages. These centres are actively participating in the national missions like IMSD, nation-wide wetland mapping, CAPE, cotton acreage and condition assessment, NRIS, etc.

North-eastern space applications centre

Preparatory works have been taken up during the year towards establishment of a North-Eastern Space Applications Centre (NE-SAC), as a joint effort of North-Eastern Council and Department of Space. NE-SAC will have facilities for remote sensing satellite communications and space science research which will be tuned towards overall developmental needs of the region and also as an initiative for establishing an institution of high-technology applications in the region.

NNRMS standing committees

NNRMS activities are guided by nine Standing Committees - Agriculture & Soils, Bio-Resources, Geology and Mineral Resources, Water Resources, Ocean Resources, Cartography and Mapping, Urban Management, Rural Development and, Technology and Training. Under the Standing Committee on Agriculture and Soils, a project on Forecasting Agriculture output using Space, Agrometeorology and Land observation (FASAL) has been taken up. As a pilot study, FASAL has been taken up in Orissa during Kharif 1998-99 for rice. In the first phase of FASAL, crop-forecasting in Kharif season for 1998 has also been carried out in Assam, Andhra Pradesh, Haryana, Orissa and Uttar Pradesh. Under the Standing Committee on Bio-Resources, biodiversity characterisation at landscape level has been taken up, covering three main biodiversity rich regions of the country, namely, North-East Himalayas, North-West Himalayas and Western Ghats. Under the Standing Committee on Water Resources, monitoring of floods in Ganga, Gangtok, Kosi, Brahmaputra and Rapti basins has been carried out.

Pilot project on creation of Geological Information System for mineral prognostics and environmental studies for parts of Maharashtra and Madhya Pradesh have been taken up under Standing Committee on Geology and Mineral Resources. Systems study for a Geological Information System for the whole country is also being worked out. Under the Standing Committee on Ocean Resources, plans have been worked out for application of data from Ocean Colour Monitor (OCM) and Multi-frequency Scanning Microwave Radiometer (MSMR) of Indian Remote Sensing satellite, IRS-P4 to be launched in 1999-2000.

Under the Standing Committee on Water Resources, identification of prospective locations for ground water exploration in over 4 lakh habitations, is proposed under Rajiv Gandhi National Drinking Water Mission. Approval has been accorded for carrying out the project in four states, Karnataka, Kerala, Rajasthan and Madhya Pradesh. Under the Standing Committee on Rural Development, a pilot study has been carried out to establish feasibility of using IRS-1C/1D data for rural development. Under Standing Committee on Urban Management, a base map updation for 23 towns using data from Panchromatic Camera of IRS has been taken up. Urban land use change and growth monitoring for major cities, master plan development f or 8 towns and metros, establishing urban information systems, infrastructure siting and perspective plan generation for Pimpri -Chinchwad area have also been taken up.

Updating topographic maps using IRS data, digital GIS data-bases standardisation and development, digital photogrammetry and ortho image generation and DEM generation, large scale mapping, etc., are being guided by the Standing Committee on Cartography and Mapping. The Standing Committee on Training and Technology has worked out a plan for organising a series of training programmes at school, university and professionals levels in different application areas of remote sensing.

Remote sensing training and education

Indian Institute of Remote Sensing (IIRS) at Dehradun is offering training in the field of remote sensing and allied areas, to both Indian and foreign participants. Besides remote sensing technology, training at IIRS includes diverse application-related subjects and user-tailored courses. In collaboration with ITC of The Netherlands, a geo-informatics laboratory has been established. NRSA, Hyderabad and RRSSCs of DOS have also conducted various training programmes in the application of remote sensing and GIS to different thematic areas for scientists and officials from various organisations.

A total of 297 scientists and officials from various organisations were trained in different disciplines during the year.

Satellite news

The most significant technical development in television news has been the introduction of electronic transmission of news pictures—a revolution that was foreseeable in the late 1950s, but did not come to full fruition until the 1970s. Foreign newsfilm coverage in particular is now no longer dependent on despatch riders and train or airline schedules; instead, communications satellites, strategically placed over the oceans, relay moving pictures almost instantaneously from one side of the world to the other to be recorded on videotape for use in the same day's news programmes. This process of electronic news transmission had begun in the 1960s with the Eurovision news exchanges among the broadcasting stations of western Europe, using land line and microwave links, and with similar hook-ups across the American continent. These were given a considerable boost by the Vietnam war, coverage of which was speeded from west to east coast, after airfreighting across the Pacific.

The first communications satellite over the Atlantic, Telstar, was used for news transmissions from 1962, when an ITN news programme was broadcast live from New York instead of from the usual London studio. It was a gimmick that made the front page lead in the following morning's papers, but within days the process of transmitting bit news stories by satellite had become, if not routine, at least unremarkable. In those early days, the satellite were in low orbits round the earth, so that they rose and set, and were available as relay stations only for about half an hour at a time whiie they were "visible" from both sides of the Atlantic. Later satellites were put in orbits 22,300 miles up, their orbital speed coinciding with the rotation of the earth, so they remained fixed over one spot, and were available permanently. There are now four such satellites-two over the Atlantic, one over the Indian Ocean, and one over the Pacific. Each satellite can cover about 40% of the earth's surface, so the link-up is now global.

To anyone without television experience a script may seem to be a bare and unimpressive piece of prose. We are so used to the literary conventions of the printed page that we forget how artificial they are. A writer for print has only the black ink patterns on the page to communicate his thought. Words must be chosen with precision and ordered with care to overcome the lack of vocal emphasis and visual expression. In television, words carry only a part of the sense; the rest is supplied by tone of voice, facial expression, music, an illustration, a film or even a pause. A television writer must learn to see the programme in terms of action and reaction of dramatic development, rather than as words on a page. He must learn to listen with his inner ear to how the script will sound when it is spoken.

> From the Palace Guardhouse, rose-pink against the snow, a fur-capped company in sale grey greatcoats

> swings off easily past frozen quays. Bright basic played on curiously elongated French horns takes them up towards the kiosked, tree-lined espanade. They steam as they march. Each man carries a rifle whose butt is of polished walnut, like a piece of elegant furniture. Ducks pause to watch them from the apron of ice, fur-clad shoppers from the bright-windows pavements.

This is an excellent piece of descriptive prose for the printed page, but for a television programme or film it would be useless. It is composed almost entirely of visual images cunningly evoked by words. On television the word images would either draw attention to the absence of pictures or if suitable pictures had been filmed-would describe only what the viewers could see for himself. This would be the major fault in the writing from a television point of view. There are others as well. Try to say easily and naturally,....fur-capped company in pale grey greatcoats. "Say the word "kiosked" to the next person you meet, and ask him what it means. It will probably be baffled. It is a word one can write, but not say. It is possible that a passage like the one above might inspire a director or cameraman to shoot a fine film sequence, but the words themselves would never be transmitted. They are literally and television is not a literary medium.

Writing for television needs to be easy and colloquial in style, for although the audience may total millions it consists at any one place of a few people in a room, and one must not address them as though they were a public meeting. The script must never seem to be written or read, but must come from the speaker in the kind of sentences that might be spoken in a room without absordity. Of course one cannot afford the looseness of real conversational speech the words must be organised with care and economy, but they must sound easy and spontaneous. They must also be written in a style that comes naturally to the person who is to speak them, particularly if he is to be in vision when they are spoken.

The writer should imagine the programmer as it will be: he should run through the titles and the opening music, picture to himself the first scene, and listen with his inward ear to the words as he writes them. Fine phrases and impressive preambles are usually a mistake: simplicity and directness rarely are.

> "*Good evening.* This Is Your Life... this is the Boat Show. But we're interested in one boat and one man..."

In 20 words the programme and the location are identified, and our curiosity is aroused. On paper, the words are sparse, even unclear, but spoken with the right emphasis over a long shot of the exhibition with the camera zooming in on the boat in question, they made perfect sense. Words in television are only part of the total communication, and are sometimes not needed at all. Not the least of a good script writer's virtues is knowing when to say nothing.

Scripting the documentary

A writer's approach to a television script differs according to the type of programme. For a film documentary, he begins with a mass of detailed research material compiled by himself or a researcher. From this and the outline treatment already agreed with the producer he must shape a story in words and images that engages and holds the audience's attention.

Although people profess to like "good documentaries," it is a fact that they want them only as an extra. But they are prepared to accept documentaries only if they crop up in an evening's viewing and happen to capture their interest. If they become at all board, they are likely to switch to more entertaining fare. For the documentary writer and producer, this is the greatest peril and challenge. A television documentary must capture its audience in the first minute, and fight for its attention for the next half hour.

The golden rule is-begin with action and with people, then make the audience curious about what happens next. If the documentary is about an airport, do not begin with a long shot of a plane landing; begin with a pilot as he starts his approach. Put the audience in the cockpit with him, in the control tower following the radar screens, in the cabin with the passengers. Let them listen to the talk down and watch the runway rushing up to meet them. Only when the plane touches down need you to a long shot of it on the runway, and bring in a line of commentary: "That happens 200 times a day at X Airport."

The action need not be wildly dramatic or on a large scale: a small boy peering through a hedge, a girl running down a flight of stairs might be good beginnings, provided the viewer is given something or someone to identify with, and is given an incentive to go on watching. Once his interest is aroused, he will tolerate a slackening of pace and tension while the scene is set for the story. Then everything depends on narrative-the stage by stage unfolding of a story, building to a climax and a conclusion. New facts, new insights, new scenes must constantly be found and presented, each one adding to the last, and advancing the story. If there is a commercial break, the first half of the film must build to a "cliff-hanger" ending that will sustain an audience's interest and curiosity until the second half. It is often a temptation. He should remember that the viewer is being bombarded with information through eyes and ears, and there is a limit to the amount he can take in without mental indigestion and consequent withdrawal of interest.

Layout of television script

The usual and most convenient way to lay out a script is to divide the page in half vertically, setting out the story line on the right, and a brief description of the pictures on the left. Inevitably, both are modified as shooting progress, and the film itself absorbs much of the written script.

Fashionable Kingston street	Only a few hundred yards from the elegant homes of London's middle class in the royal Borough of Chelsea and Kingston lie some of the worst slums in Britain.
Small boy runs down street	Interior-various shots of slum house-one sink on landing-family of five in one room
Interior—various shots of slum house—one sink on landing—family of five in one room	The Smith family of Blank Street-five of them-live in one room. Their only source of water a tap on the landing, their only source of heat a paraffin stove. When it rains, the water comes in, when it blows, the wind howls through the cracks in the window.

In the final version of the film, most if not all of these words might well be unnecessary. The director might begin with an interior shot of a rich household, and looking out. Below, in the street, a poor child walks past with a loaf of bread under his arm, past the "FOR SALE 130,000" sign outside one house, round the corner to the dilapidated building where he lives. The camera follows him up the uncarpeted stairs, past the dripping tap on the landing to the crowded square of the one room, where a baby is tugging at washing hanging round a paraffin stove. The point of the script is made without words. But without the words in the fist place, the sequence might never have been shot.

Many of the facts set down in the script may eventually be covered in interviews during the film, or in voice-over narration edited from tape recordings of people appearing in the film. Sometimes, the narration may be done entirely in this way, with the script consisting of various voices edited together to form a continuous story line. Inevitably, the writer's work becomes submerged and absorbed in that of the producer, the director, the cameraman and the film editor. So much so that documentary writers often move into producing or directing their own films-or producers and directors write them in the first place.

The writer's final job on a film documentary is to write the commentary. This is a curious technical skill that needs a good deal of experience before it can be done well. The trick is to the film itself tell as much as possible, using commentary covers more than half of a documentary film, there is something seriously wrong with either the film or the writing. Timing is of the essence. Words and pictures must work together, often to the split second, for the best effect. This imposes a stern discipline on sentence construction. Dominating everything is the footage-or timing-of-each scene and sequence. These words take up one second, two words one 35 mm foot, five words one 16 mm foot-more or less. It is useless to try to cram in more words than there is time for, or to anticipate with the commentary what the film will reveal in its own good time. Film has its own pace and logic, sometimes faster than words, sometimes slower, and the commentary must follow it. Cutting film to match words is possible, but it never works for long. The picture is naturally dominant.

Scene	*Cumulative footage*	*Individual footage*
LS Cairo and River Nile	5	5
LS Crowded bridge, pan to LS of boat sailing down river	11	6
Aerial shot of cultivation round river with desert round	15	4
LS river bank from boat	19	4
LS ruined temple	19	4
LS ruined temple	22	3
Tilt up pillars to low-angle shot of them against sky	27	5
Another angle, ditto	29	2
MS bas relief on wall of hunting scene	32	3
CJ details of bas relief	36	4
LS barren hill tilt down to group of tourists entering tomb	41	5
LS interior of tomb as tourists enter	44	3
LS ciffin of King Tut	48	4
CJ face on coffin	53	5
LS coffin, tilt up to wall painting	59	6

The commentary writer works with a shot list prepared from the final cut of the film. This sets down a brief description of each shot with a note of its length in feet or seconds, according to taste or studio custom. The following example is listed in 16 mm feet:

This is obviously a travelogue type of film with no strong action to carry the story line. The commentary will have to work hard to give significance to the shots, which are only mildly illustrative of the theme-the economic development of Egypt. The following commentary is fairly pedestrian, but is at last calculated to make the most of words and pictures together. The figures on the left mark the footage at which the commentator will start to speak either cueing himself or being cued with the aid of the footage counter in the dubbing theatre.

— Four hundred and fifty years before Christ, a Greek historian described Egypt as "the gift of the Nile." / Today, a nation of thirty million people still depends on the river for its existence.

— It brings a narrow ribbon / of life to what would otherwise be total desolation. /

— Five thousand years ago, this long fertile valley gave birth to one of the world's / most advanced civilisations. Here, the earth yielded enough for man to stop struggling for mere / existence, and start reaching for the stars.

— To the Ancient Egyptians, life seemed so rich and good that they tried to carry it with them beyond the / grave. Here in the Valley of the Kings, in 1922, the English archaeologist Howard Carrier discovered a tomb which had remained untouched for three / thousand three hundred years-the tomb of the young King Tut-ankh-Amun. /

— His mummified body lay inside four coffins of cedar of / Lebanon, entirely covered with gold. "In the whole history of excavation" -wrote Carter- "nothing so wondrous had been seen as was now revealed by an / electric torch."

A great deal of more thought and calculation has gone into this simple bit of commentary than might appear at first sight. Note that it does not begin until the audience has been given time to take in the first picture then, in the first sentence, it identifies the city and the river while at the same time emphasising the historical theme which will be developed later.

The reference to 30 million people falls on the shot of crowded bridge. The words "narrow ribbon" slightly precede the aerial shot showing the narrow ribbon so that the audience is prepared to see the picture that way when it is presented. The metaphor about reaching for the stars coincides with the camera tilt upwards. Pauses are left between the paragraphs to give the viewer time to take in words and picture, and make the connection between the two. Every sentence relates in some way to the picture on the screen at that time without wasting time and words in describing what the viewers can see for himself.

The only way to write a commentary closely to film is to count words and calculate footages precisely. Often, a sentence or a paragraphs will have to be re-written several times before it "hits" the picture in the right way. Extra words may be necessary to pad out a sentence so that the key word coincides with a certain image or action; at other times, the wordage may have to be cut to the bone for the same reason. Sentences may have to be inverted and turned inside out.

If a film shows a long shot of a crowd of demonstrators, then a close shot of a particular personality waving a banner, it is no use following the normal subject-verb-object sentence construction: "Professor John Snudge, Head of the English Department, was among the demonstrators." This will only irritate the viewer by causing him to look for Snudge when there is no Snudge yet to be seen. When Snudge does finally appear, the viewer will be uncertain whether that is, in fact, he. Far better to turn the sentence round, and write: "Among the demonstrators was the Head of the English Department, / Professor John Snudge." This sentence would be "back-timed" from the shot of Snudge so that the first part of it coincide with the long shot of the demonstrators, and the mention of Snudge's name with the close shot. Not only does this identify the man positively, it also alerts the viewer, in advance, to what he is about to see. Phrases like "as you can see" or "this is" or "in the picture now" are never necessary in film commentary. If words and picture coincide, the viewer will make the connection. Equally, if they don't he will be baffled-and less than a second's error can make all the difference.

This automatic link between what is said and seen is rich in opportunities as well as pitfalls for the writer. Words and pictures together can counterpoint each other, offering metaphors, irony and allusions that neither would have separately. In a documentary series about the World War II, there was an episode about the protracted struggle against the U-boats in the Atlantic. It ended with a long shot out to sea with a smudge of smoke on the horizon. The commentary line was: "But victory was still hull down on the horizon." In a film about prospecting for oil and gas in the North Sea, the commentary referred to the roulette table odds against a major discovery, and spoke of oil companies placing their million-pound bets, over shots of men gathered round chequer-boarded charts and aerial views of drilling rigs in the sea. Used with skill, words and pictures can multiply each other's impact, but one needs to be wary of being too facile. Once the words attract attention to themselves instead of to the picture and the story, the game is being overplayed. The picture must be dominant.

Writing newsfilm commentary

Writing commentary to newsfilm is governed by the same principles, but plagued with special problems. Newsfilm is not shot to a script, and often covers only a part of the story that must be told. It is shot in a hurry, edited in a rush, leaving the writer little time to polish his sentences. Nevertheless, he must turn in a workmanlike job, and with practice this is usually possible. Normally, he sees the rushes when they are screened, and gives his opinion about which shots will be needed to put his story across. Often, he goes into the cutting room with the film editor, and works out the sequences with him, particularly if there are passages of sound film-a speech or an interview-to cut but that requires a newsman's editorial judgement.

Although the film may tell or illustrate only a part of the story, the news writer's duty is to tell the whole, sometimes over shots which are not directly relevant to the facts he must put across. Film of a road accident rarely shows the actual collision. Film of an international conference may well show only representatives coming and going from the conference hall, while the writer must contrive to convey what the conference is about and what is thought to have transpired behind the closed doors.

As always, the trick is to relate the spoken word to the picture. The usual form is to write a paragraph of introduction to be delivered by the newscaster in vision. This follows the normal journalistic practice of presenting the main facts of the story in an arresting and lucid fashion. Then comes the film, and a different style has to be followed. The opening words of commentary must tell the viewer where and when the film was shot and must convey the rest of the news while keying it to the picture on the screen.

Agencies the main news source

The information for the commentary is culled from the cameraman's dope sheet, news cuttings from the library and news agency copy. The news agency wire services are the basis of a television news programme. Twenty-four hours a day, the teleprinters of the Press Association, Reuters, Associated Press and others chatter out thousands of words, providing a blanket coverage of home and foreign news.

In America, the wire services send a special news summary to the hundred of broadcasting stations across the country who report national as well as local news. In Britain, where local stations give only local news, the two national services from London-ITN and BBC-take the same agency material as the Fleet Street newspapers, but they use it differently. Newspapers regard the agencies as background and filler material, relying for their main coverage on their own reporters, but television does not use its reporters in this way-as news-gatherers and writers-and agency copy is the staple material of news broadcasts.

It is rarely possible to use agency copy on the air in the form that it comes over the machines. An agency's main function is to pump out the news as fast as it can for the benefit of its main subscribers, with little regard to the special needs of television. Different reporters' stories on the same subject are strung together with small concern for quality of writing, and sent to all subscribers for them to edit as they wish. For television, this usually means a total rewrite. Out of several hundreds of words, the television sub-editor must extract the essentials for a story only twenty or thirty seconds long.

Writing for speech

The requirements are accuracy, clarity and brevity. The story must be completely understandable at first hearing. If the audience are muddled or mystified, you have lost their attention for the next few seconds at least, and that is enough to lose their interest altogether. The newspaper reader is eased into a story by the headline and the dateline. By the time he reads the text he already has a good idea of subject, place and personalities.

> The wave of "sightings" of unidentified flying objects sweeping the world since the Christmas photographs of "flying saucers" from New Zealand reached a fresh peak yesterday-in actual "landing"
>
> A former nurse in South Africa claimed to have encountered a pink unidentified object. She said it landed near her home, and a squad of strange darkskinned little men got out.
>
> Mrs. Meagan Quezet, of Krugersdorp, west of Johannesburg, said the incident happened just after midnight, when she took her 12-year-old son, Andre, for a walk because he could not sleep.
>
> "As we walked down the road we could see a bright pink light over a rise, and suddenly we came across this thing standing in the road about 20 yards away. In front of it were these five or six beings.
>
> "These people were darkish skinned as far as I could tell. One of the men had a beard, and seemed to be the leader. I said hello to one of them but I couldn't understand what he was

> saying. The creatures jumped about five feet into the air and vanished through a door into their craft. Then with a humming noise it disappeared into the sky."
>
> Mrs. quezet and her son gave identical descriptions of the craft.

This kind of writing, adequate for the printed page, turns to a blur of confusing words when spoken. Stripped of headline and dateline, the story gives no clue about location until after the first sentence. The words sound awkward and unnatural on the tongue, and there is too much disparate information to take in at a first hearing. A television treatment of the same story might go like this:

> Another report of an unidentified flying object-from South Africa-and this time it's said to have landed.
>
> A former nurse, taking her 12-year-old son out for a walk just after midnight, says she saw a pink object in the road near home outside Johannesburg. A squad of dark-skinned little men got out, she said. When she spoke to one she did not understand his reply. The beings then jumped back into their craft, which took off and vanished.

The woman's son is reported to have given an identical description of the UFO.

Like most television news stories, this one condenses into 45 seconds what might easily occupy up to half a column in a newspaper. A whole half hour news programme can contain only about 4000 words; not as much as the front page of most newspapers-and yet the main news must be covered. A newspaper can afford to print much that will not interest everyone. Each reader can select, accept or reject what is in the paper. If, after reading headline and intro, he finds that a story does not interest him, he can turn to something else with no break in the general activity of reading the paper. But in television he can not skip back and forth through the columns and the pages; he must take what is given as it comes. The television audience is much larger, than the circulation of any one newspaper, and includes readers of both the "popular" and "quality" Press. Both must be served and satisfied, their interest awakened and held. Here, the enforced brevity of television news is a help. No story needs to go on long enough to become a bore to any large section of the audience, and if the stories are well enough written as a normal practice the viewer will come to know that his time will not be wasted by superfluous detail, and he will often follow a story on television that he would not bother to read in a newspaper. But the writing must be simple, lucid and easy on the ear. A story book once used by ITN, London, put it like this:

> A well-written ITN programme sounds clear, intelligent, friendly and authoritative at once. Though space is limited, good writing is tremendously important. Don't be frightened to be dramatic in your writing, if the story merits it. But try to secure your drama by facts, not by adjectives. The fact Mrs Kennedy cried out "No, no!" when Kennedy was shot is of more value than a dozen adjectives. But adjectives can be useful too, provided they are appropriate, and the kind you would use in spoken speech. Sentences should be kept short and simple, and must be completely comprehensible at first hearing. The viewer, until the reader, cannot pause to refer back or to digest a point. The simple pattern of subject, verb, object usually fits television speech best. Not every sentence needs to be complete, and the verb can be omitted surprisingly often.

In the BBC, news sub-editors are expected to dictate their

stories to a typist to ensure that they think only in terms of the spoken word. Other news services do not run to such luxuries, but the principle is a valuable one. A writer can still utter his sentences to himself before committing them on to paper, and the more he does it from his own mind and not from the news agency copy, better the results are likely to be. Facts and figures can always be double checked afterwards. In tackling a complicated story, a useful technique is to read the agency copy thoroughly until you have understood it perfectly, then put it to one side and decide how you would tell the story to your wife or drinking companion. Almost unconsciously, the mind recalls the salient facts first. In speech, one often uses an alerting phrase before telling a story- "Have you heard about house prices? They've gone up by 20 per cent".

Broadcast news follow the same pattern: "A big increase in house prices. The Nationwide Building Society says the average price of houses in the south-east has gone up by 20 per cent in the past six months."

Often, this "headline" trick of speech can be used to tickle the audience's curiosity a little before giving the full story:

> "A last-minute entry for the big race tomorrow..."
>
> "Good news for car-owners..."

Phrases of this kind are useful, too, in pointing a change of subject from the last story.

While learning to listen to his writing, the news writer must learn to visualise it. The total communication is what matters, and that includes picture. If a still or a map or a diagram can make things clearer, then use it, and write the story round it so that words and picture complement each other. Individual newscasters have their own style of delivery, not only in vocal intonation, but in facial expression and gesture. One can hit this off by imagining the story as it will look and sound on the air. With experience, it can seem that one is not so much writing a piece as taking it down from dictation over one's mental television set.

For the dedicated writer who likes or has a compulsion to the lonely business of putting words on paper, television can be a frustrating medium. It scatters words on the air, and loses them forever. It transmutes lively writing into images and action, giving the glamour and the credit to performer and director. The writer seems to be regarded as a mere word technician. But the kind of mind that makes a good programme is a writer's mind, and television can not live without them. Perhaps it should value them more highly.

4

Important Projects and Technology Development

Department of Space undertakes projects to design, develop and operate satellites and launch vehicles to provide space services in a self-reliant manner. Details of important DOS projects and the progress made under them are as follows.

Indian National Satellite System (INSAT)

INSAT system was established in 1983 with the launch of INSAT-113, for providing telecommunications, television broadcasting, meteorology, disaster warning and distress alert services. INSAT is a joint venture of the Department of Space (DOS), Department of Telecommunications, India Meteorological Department, All India Radio and Doordarshan. DOS is responsible for establishment and operation of INSAT space segment. INSAT space segment at present consists of five satellites - INSAT-1D, the last of the INSAT-1 series launched in 1990, three ISRO-built satellites, INSAT-2A launched in July 1992, INSAT-2B launched in July 1993 and INSAT-2C December 1995 and INSAT-2DT acquired from ARABSAT Organisation.

INSAT-2E

INSAT-2E is the last of INSAT-2 series of satellites built by ISRO. It is scheduled for launch by the European launch vehicle, Ariane, from Kourou in French Guyana in early 1999. It will carry 17 C-band and lower extended

C-band transponders, a VHRR similar to that of INSAT-2A and INSAT-2B but with an additional water vapour channel, and a Charge Coupled Device (CCD) camera operating in visible, near infrared and shortwave infrared bands with 1 km resolution.

During the year, assembly, integration and testing of INSAT-2E at spacecraft level has been completed and after thermovacuum and thermal balance tests, as well as, vibration and acoustic tests, it is now ready for transportation to Kourou.

INSAT-3 series

Five satellites - INSAT-3A through INSAT-3E are planned to be built under INSAT-3 series. INSAT-3A, INSAT-3B and INSAT-3C communication payloads are planned to augment the INSAT transponder capacity to cater to the increased demand of about 130 transponders by the year 2002. INSAT-3A will carry full complement of meteorological payloads - VHRR and CCD camera similar to INSAT-2E and a DRT (Data Relay Transponder) and a SAS&R (Satellite Aided Search and Rescue) transponders - besides communication transponders - twelve in C-band, six in extended C-band and six in Ku-band. INSAT-3B will not have meteorological payloads and will carry communication payloads comprising 12 transponders in extended C-band, three in Ku-band and one S-band Mobile Satellite Service (MSS) transponder. INSAT-3C will also be a communication satellite carrying 24 C-band transponders, six extended C-band transponders, two S-band transponders and one S-band MSS transponders. INSAT-31) is planned as a meteorological satellite carrying an advanced SIX-channel imager, a nineteen-channel sounder and transponder for meteorological data relay and satellite aided search and rescue. Configuration of INSAT-3E is under finalisation. INSAT-3A and INSAT-3B are planned for launch during 1999-2000 with the launch of INSAT-3B preceding that of INSAT-3A in order to meet the requirement of extended C-band capacity at the earliest.

During the year, preliminary design review of INSAT-3A has been completed and the configuration finalised. Subsystems fabrication has commenced. Detailed design review of all subsystems of INSAT-3B have also been completed. Integration and testing of propulsion systems have been completed and integration of telemetry and telecommand packages initiated.

For INSAT-3C, payload and spacecraft configurations have been finalised and fabrication of subsystems that are common with INSAT-3A and INSAT-3B initiated. INSAT-31) payload and spacecraft configuration are under finalisation. Design options for the INSAT-3E bus are being studied.

GSAT

The developmental test flights of Geosynchronous Satellite Launch Vehicle (GSLV) will be used to launch GSAT satellites which are intended for conducting experiments/demonstration of advanced communication technologies like digital audio, data and video broadcasting, internet services and wide-band multimedia with on-board processors as well as to prove, in flight, advanced spacecraft hardware. GSAT-1, planned for launch on board GSLV-Dl during 1999-2000 will carry two S-band transponders, a high power C-band transponder and two indigenously developed C-band transponders.

Detailed design review of GSAT-1 has been completed. Integration of propulsion tanks with spacecraft structure has also been completed during the year and subsystems are in various stages of fabrication and testing. Configuration of GSAT-2, to be launched by the second developmental flight of GSLV, is under finalisation.

Indian Remote Sensing Satellite (IRS)

IRS system was commissioned with the launch of IRS-1A in March 1988. IRS system at present consists of four ISRO-built satellites, IRS-113 launched in August 1991, IRS-IC launched in December 1995, IRS-113 launched in September 1997 and IRS-P3 launched in March 1996. IRS-113, like its predecessor IRS-1A, carries two types of cameras, LISS-1 and LISS-11, with spatial resolutions of 72.5 m and 36.25 m, respectively. LISS-1 has a swath of 148 km and the two LISS-11 cameras have a composite swath of 148 km.

IRS-1C and IRS-1D are identical and have enhanced capabilities compared to IRS-1A and IRS-1B in terms of spatial resolution, additional spectral bands, stereoscopic imaging, wide field coverage and revisit capabilities. They carry tape-recorder for collecting data even when the satellites are not visible to any of the ground stations. These satellites carry three cameras on board: (i) a Panchromatic camera (PAN), which is a high resolution camera operating in Panchromatic band with a resolution of 5.8 rn and swath of 70 km; it can be steered up to + 26 degree across-track, thus enabling stereoscopic imagery and better revisit capability; (ii) a Linear Imaging Self-scanning Sensor (LISS-III) operating in four spectral bands - three in Visible/Near Infrared (VNIR) and one in Short Wave Infrared (SWIR) ranges. It provides a ground resolution of 23.5 in VNIR band and 70.5 m in the SWIR band with swaths of 141 km and 148 km, respectively; (iii) a Wide Field Sensor (WiFS), a coarse resolution (188.3 m) camera covering a wide swath of 810 km.

IRS-P3, which was launched by India's PSLV during the third developmental flight, carries two remote sensing payloads - a Wide Field Sensor (WiFS) similar to that of IRS-1C but with an additional Short Wave Infrared Band (SWIR), a Modular Opto-electronic

Scanner (MOS) of the German Space Agency (DLR). Apart from remote sensing payloads, IRS-P3 also carries an X-ray astronomy payload.

IRS-P4 (OCEANSAT)

An ocean remote sensing satellite, IRS-P4, carrying Ocean Colour Monitor (OCM).and a IRS-PS (CARTOSAT) Multifrequency Scanning Microwave Radiometer (MSMR), is planned for launch during 1999-2000 on board PSLV-C2. OCM is a solid state camera operating in push broom scanning mode, using linear array Charge Coupled Devices (CCD) as detectors for generating ocean biological parameters. OCM provides a resolution of 360 metre with a swath of 1420 km. It operates in eight very near infrared bands. It will be placed in 720 km polar orbit and provide a repetivity of 2 days for the coverage.

During the year all the main-frame systems, earth sensors and digital sensor have been realised and integrated. The payloads are in an advanced stage of fabrication and testing.

IP.S-P5 (Cartosat)

IRS-P5, planned for launch during 2000-01 is intended for cartographic applications. It will carry two Panchromatic cameras with 2.5 metre spatial resolution and a swath of 30 km. The cameras provide stereo imageries useful for generation of digital terrain models. It will also carry a solid state recorder for storing payload data. The orbit plan for this satellite is 617 km polar sunsynchronous orbit and it can provide a revisit capability of 5 days.

During the year, preliminary design review for the subsystems as well as at spacecraft level has been completed. Fabrication of mechanical and electronic packages has also been initiated. The electro-optic module design and optimisation has also been carried out and fabrication initiated.

IRS-P6 (resourcesat)

IRS-P6 is intended to continue the services of IRS-II). It is planned to be launched during 2001-02. It will carry a multispectral camera LISS-III similar to that of IRS-1C and IRS-113 and in addition a high resolution multispectral camera, LISS-IV which can provide a resolution of better than six metre. An Advanced Wide Field Sensor (AWFS) with a spatial resolution of 70 metre in three spectral bands and a swath of 400 km will also be included. This will be placed in a sunsynchronous polar orbit of 817 km. During the year procurement of materials and components has been initiated. Payload definitions and details of spacecraft bus have been studied.

Stretched Rohini Satellite Series (SROSS)

The 113 kg SROSS-C2 satellite, launched by ASLV-D4 on May 4, 1994 carries two scientific payloads, a Gamma-Ray Burst (GRB) experiment and a Retarding Potential Analyser (RPA). Both the payloads continued to provide valuable scientific data during the year.

Launch vehicle technology

Launch Vehicle development is directed towards achieving self-reliance in placing Indian satellites in the required orbits. While development of Polar Satellite Launch Vehicle, PSLV, capable of placing 1,200 kg class Indian Remote Sensing (IRS) satellites into 820 km Polar sun-synchronous orbit has already been completed, development of Geosynchronous Satellite Launch Vehicle, GSLV, capable of launching 2,000-2,500 kg INSAT class of satellites into Geosynchronous Transfer Orbit (GTO), has made substantial progress during the year.

Polar Satellite Launch Vehicle (PSLV)

PSLV is the first operational satellite launch vehicle of India. The first operational flight of this vehicle, PSLV-C1, was conducted on September 29,1997 when it placed the Indian Remote Sensing satellite, IRS-11), in a polar orbit.

With a lift-off weight of about 294 tonne and measuring 44 m in height, PSLV is capable of placing 1,200 kg payload in 817 km polar sunsynchronous orbit. It has four stages. The first stage is of 2.8 m diameter and has 138 tonne of solid propellant. Six solid propellant strap-on motors each with 9 tonne are attached to the first stage. The 2.8 in diameter liquid propulsion second stage carries 40.6 tonne of propellant. The third stage is a 7.2 tonne solid propellant motor and the fourth stage is again a liquid propellant motor with 2 tonne of propellant. PSLV incorporates closed-loop guidance with an on-board processor.

Launch of the second operational flight, PSLV-C2, is planned for 1999-2000 and it will carry on board three satellites, Indian Remote Sensing satellite, IRS-P4, as the primary payload and a Korean micro satellite KITSAT and a German micro satellite, TUBSAT, as piggybacks. PSLV-C3 and PSLV-C4 are planned for launch during 2000-01 and 2001-02 carrying IRS-P5 and IRS-P6 respectively.

During the year, post-flight analysis of PSLV-C1 has been concluded and the under-performance of fourth stage in this flight has been investigated. Malfunction of pressure regulation system of the stage has been established through ground simulation tests and corrective actions implemented for PSLV-C2 flight. Subassemblies for the PSLV-C2 have reached an advanced stage of readiness. Mechanical and electrical integration of all subsystems have been completed and phase-I tests and vibration tests of subassemblies conducted. Stage integration and testing and vehicle assembly at launch pad are being initiated.

Fabrication of hardware for PSLV-C3 has commenced. Development activities related to variants of PSLV have also been initiated during the year.

Geosynchronous Satellite Launch Vehicle (GSLV)

Development of GSLV has been undertaken to achieve capability to launch 2,500 kg class of communication satellites into geosynchronous transfer orbit. GSLV is a three stage vehicle - the first stage employs a 129 tonne solid propellant core motor with four liquid propellant strap-ons with a loading of 40 tonne each. The second stage is a liquid propulsion system with a propellant loading of 37.5 tonne and the upper stage is a cryogenic engine with a loading of 12 tonne using liquid oxygen and liquid hydrogen.

The first developmental flight of GSLV is planned during 1999-2000.

Development and qualification of all systems, specifically developed for GSLV, have been completed during the year. Substantial progress has been made towards assembly and integration of different stages for the first developmental test flight, GSLV-D1.

Liquid propellant strap-on stage (L-40) qualification test, strap-on nose cone structural test and ground resonance test (GRT) with one L-40, have been major accomplishments during the year. All four flight stages of L-40 are getting ready. Full scale heatshield functional tests have also been completed. All the avionics packages for the prototype equipment bay have been realised and flight packages are in various stages of integration and test. Pogo analysis, slosh analysis for up-dated GSLV baffle configurations for all liquid propulsion stages and studies on GS-2 jet impingement on interstages during separation have been carried out.

The first cryogenic flight stage has been received from Russia and positioned in SHAR Centre.

Configuration studies for advanced versions of GSLV is continuing.

Cryogenic Upper Stage Project (CUSP)

The CUSP envisages design and development of a cryogenic upper stage for use in GSLV for flights beyond 1999-2000. It will have a thrust of 7.5 tonne and carries 12.5 tonne propellant (liquid oxygen and liquid hydrogen). The stage which bums for 800 sec will have a diameter of 2.8 m and measure about 9 m in length.

The thrust chamber has been tested for 50 seconds under derated conditions during the year. The main test facilities have undergone acceptance tests.

Sounding rockets

ISRO has developed a series of sounding rockets for conducting atmospheric research and other scientific investigations. Three Rohini sounding rockets RH-560 Mk-II were launched during the year from SHAR Centre, Sriharikota, carrying scientific payloads developed by German and other European space science laboratories. The payloads were intended to study the dynamics of equatorial ionosphere during the occurrence of Spread-F phenomena. Three RH-200 rockets with meteorological payloads were flown from Thumba and ten RH-200 rockets prepared for launch. Qualification of RH-300 Mk-II rocket for low temperature environments is underway.

Aerodynamic tests for an air-breathing rocket have also been conducted during the year. A liquid kerosene fuel feed system for the rocket has been developed and the ejector rocket sub scale tests completed. Preliminary design of Ejector Ram Jet Vehicle (ERJV) has been made and drawings generated. Preliminary grain configuration has also been made.

Technology development

Development of various technologies required for INSAT and IRS satellites, launch vehicles, associated ground systems as well as to conduct application missions are carried out in different centres of DOS. Technology development covers a number of disciplines and are synergised to realise operational space systems. Highlights of technology developments carried out during the year are covered in the following paragraphs.

Aeronautics

Aerodynamics and flight mechanics studies on various configurations for PSLV variants have been studied during the year. Aerodynamic characteristics of GSLV variants have also been studied.

Jet load and acoustic level estimation have been carried out for the second launch pad at SHAR Centre. Pre-flight and post-flight performance analysis for RH-560 Mk-II have been completed during the year. Wind-biased trajectory design has been carried out for PSLV-C2 for its launch in different months. Studies on separation dynamics of Korean KITSAT and German TUBSAT to be flown along with IRS-P4 on board PSLV-C2 have also been conducted.

In the applied mathematics area, assessment of long-term recontact possibility of multiple satellites and spent upper stage of PSLV has been estimated under various flight dispersion. Other studies in this area include aerodynamic characteristics of air-breathing rocket, flow visualisation for jet deflector for the second launch pad at SHAR and towards payload recovery.

Avionics

Major activities under avionics during the year were directed towards qualification of on-board hardware and software modules for telemetry, tracking, telecommand and inertial guidance systems for GSLV All avionic packages have been realised for PSLV-C2 flight. Fabrication and testing of flight and standby units for GSLV-D1 flight and continuation flights of PSLV are in various stages. Efforts are being made towards maintaining maximal amount of commonality for various Telemetry, Tracking and Command (TTC) packages of PSLV and GSLV for ease of fabrication and testing. Efforts towards miniaturisation of base band and RF systems is continuing. Development of a versatile software programmable Remote Unit has made significant progress during the year.

Instrumentation and telemetry systems, essential for ground qualification of GSLV cryogenic stage and L-40 stages have been developed. Qualification of data storage unit has been completed which enables delayed transmission of telemetry data of GSLV during the absence of radio visibility of the vehicle. Development of a new P-band transmitter has been completed for Rohini Sounding Rockets. Miniaturised centralised encoders have been flown in the RH-560 Mk-II flights conducted during the year. Development of a digital receiver has also made significant progress.

Qualification models of a bit-slice version of an on-board computer have undergone design and performance validation. Interface packages like bus monitoring unit and bus extender modules are also being developed for induction of new computers into launch vehicle flights. Checkout systems for testing on-board computers is under development.

In the spacecraft area, development of integrated TTC and communication network is nearing completion. A data compression system, using both lossy and loss-less techniques, to cater to the requirement of future IRS satellites is under development. Development of a solid state recorder for use in future IRS satellites has been taken up. A new generation of command encoders and station processor has been designed. Digital demodulator algorithms for high bit rate command system have been developed.

Development of a 35 kW power handling ultra low sidelobe antenna has been completed and tested at sub panel level.

In the field of spacecraft control systems, a multiprocessor configuration has been designed to meet increased computational power requirement for on-board attitude and orbit determination using star sensor. Applications software for Attitude and Orbit Control Electronics (AOCE) for IRS-P5 simulation has been completed. Software simulation for other subsystems is in progress. Computer simulation for a typical space rendezvous and docking system is another activity completed during the year. Studies on algorithms for modelling of Global Positioning System (GPS) measurements, attitude determination algorithms, kinematics and dynamics of satellite attitude, observability aspects, visibility checks and satellite selection have also been conducted during the year.

Civil engineering

Some of the major civil works completed during the year include building for spacecraft component processing facility for IISU, construction of office space for LPSC at Valiamala, construction of building for LEOS, Bangalore, construction of additional satellite control earth station at MCF, Hassan, storage building for cryogenic and L-40 stages and storage building for PS-1 and PS-0 hardware at SHAR Centre and construction of MIC Laboratory Facility at SAC, Ahmedabad.

Construction of a hostel for SHAR Centre, structural testing facility and augmentation of some of the facilities for VSSC is in progress.

Developmental communication

Major activities under developmental communications during the year, were related to Jhabua Development Communications Project (JDCP), Training and Development Communication Channel (TDCC), Social Science Research, Programme Production and Systems Studies.

Efforts continued during the year to introduce new technologies and applications in TDCC/JDCP networks. Experimentation in digital audio broadcasting and data broadcasting has been initiated. It is proposed to augment the existing network with digital transmission for broadcast and training. Talk-back channel will also be made digital at the new talk-back terminal. The existing 12 JDCP talk-back terminals, which currently operate with analog modulation will be progressively converted to digital.

Programme productions are being undertaken in various areas like watershed, health, Panchayati Raj, education, social issues and other developmental fields. Programme transmission includes regular transmission of Jhabua local and Bhopal Doordarshan news. Emphasis is put on participatory and local issues programmes. So far, around 85 talk-back training sessions have been held and more than 8,000 participants trained. 780 in-house programmes, and about 525 programmes using private agencies have been produced, a majority of them in the field with involvement of people.

Social Research has been conducted in the formative, process and summative equation of the Jhabua project. Pre-transmission survey indicated that the overall level of general knowledge was very low, about 46 percent had never viewed TV before JDCP and a majority of the respondents never participated in the Gram Sabha. Mid-transmission survey indicated that there is a high awareness and increase in the respondents who discussed about JDCP programmes, average attendance was 45 persons per location and many of them also watched JDCP inter-active (talk-back) programmes. Detailed analysis has revealed that more than 75 percent of the viewers regularly watched the programmes, and about 50 percent of them found them useful and got some new information. Overall impact of JDCP has been that there is an increase in farm produce, general awareness and also resulted in less drinking. Social research studies have also been conducted of the TDCC during 1998-99 involving several other agencies like Indira Gandhi National Open University. Further studies planned include, observational feedback, managerial, costeffectiveness, model building, pedagogical.

System studies to replicate JDCP/TDCC configurations are being taken up for Orissa, Andhra Pradesh, Tamil Nadu, etc.

Electr-optics and sensors

Main activities, during the year, in the area of electro-optics were related to realisation of INSAT-2E VHRR and CCD payloads and IRS-P4 camera payloads. Studies to define major parameters of advanced WiFS in IRS-P6 has been carried out. Design, analysis, development and came qualification of flight model camera electronics of Ocean Colour Monitor (OCM) payload for IRS-P4 have been carried out. Ground checkout instrumentation comprising PC-based spacecraft interface simulators, payload status indicators, payload evaluation units and computerised payload checkout system have also been developed for quantitative evaluation of OCM. Configuration options of camera electronics and interfaces for the IRS-P5 (CARTOSAT) have been worked out. Preliminary design review has been completed. The design and development of Microwave Sensors Payload for IRS-P4 has been completed during the year and the system integration completed. Ground checkout unit software has also been completed.

For INSAT-2E meteorological payloads, flight models of camera electronics for Very High Resolution Radiometer (VHRR) and three band CCD based payload have been tested and integrated. Development, test and evaluation of all checkout instruinentation to evaluate VHRR and CCD camera payloads have been realised. A computer-aided meteorological payload evaluation system along with its hardware interface unit has been developed. Design of INSAT-3A meteorological payload electronics has been finalised and fabrication initiated for electronics. Preliminary configuration of the camera electronics for INSAT-31) meteorological Imager and Sounder has been worked out during the year

All sensors for INSAT-2E have also been fabricated and tested during the year. They include scanning earth sensors, different types of sun sensors and temperature and pressure sensors. The sensor have since been integrated with the satellite. Dual cone earth sensor and microprocessor based digital sun sensors have been developed for IRS-P4 Fabrication and testing of digital sun sensor has been completed while dual cone earth sensor is undergoing life test. Sensors for GSAT-1 have been fabricated. Fibre optics gyro and fast attitude recovery star sensor have been developed for the first time for use in GSAT Fabrication of sensors for INSAT-3B and INSAT-3A satellites have also been in progress Fabrication of advanced optics for CARTOSAT satellite and IRS-P6 has also been initiated.

Development of a miniature earth sensor using Application Specific Integrated Circuits (ASICs) and hybrid micro electronics has been completed. A pyroelectric detector based earth sensor is under development. Development of micro mechanical systems based sensors have been initiated to reduce size and weight of spacecraft sensors. Development of near infrared band optics for LISS-III camera for IRS-P6, advanced Wide Field Sensors (WiFS) optics and optical test systems has been taken up. Design of a one metre diameter telescope has been completed. Batch production and qualification of thermistor bolometer detectors are also in progress. Development of high accuracy optical encoders, focal plane optical filters and scan mechanism for earth sensors are the other developmental activities undertaken during the year.

In the optics area, development of an RC telescope to provide spatial resolution of 1 km CCD camera of INSAT-2E has been a major effort. Fabrication of Telescope optics for panchromatic camera of IRS-P5 (CARTOSAT) is another major activity. A number of optical elements have been fabricated for star sensors, LISS-III camera and WiFS lens, optical masks for sun sensors, optical filters encoders etc. Development of metal mirrors like nickel coated beryllium optics for VHRR scan mirror and nickel coated aluminium mirror for earth sensors have been undertaken. New optical coatings have been developed for spacecraft applications like IR high reflective coating for VHRR optics, beryllium optics, special filters, and anti-reflection coating for imaging and star sensor optics.

Inertial systems

Redundant Strapdown Inertial Navigation System (RESINS) and Rate Gyro Package (RGP) for PSLV-CZ/IRS-P4 mission, simulation and protomodel of RESINS, Rate Gyro Package (RGP) and new checkout units for GSLV and inertial components for INSAT-2E and INSAT-3B have been realised during the year. Development of a vibrating beam accelerometer has been taken up. Design and configuration of metallic hemispherical resonator gyroscope has been finalised and hardware realisation initiated. 3-axis rate gyro package have been realised for PSLV-C2 and GSLV simulation purpose during the year.

Reaction Wheels, Solar Array Drives, Antenna Scan Mechanism, Inertial Reference Unit, Payload tilt mechanism and Pyro Electronics for IRS-P4 have been realised. Fabrication and testing of Momentum Wheels, Solar Array Drive and Inertial Reference Unit, VHRR Scanning Mechanism for INSAT-2E have also been completed and fabrication of these systems for INSAT-3B, INSAT-3A and GSAT is in progress.

Development of magnetic suspension reaction wheels, high torque reaction wheels for CARTOSAT, miniature IRU and HRG based IRU is continuing. Qualification tests on an alternate lubricant has also been completed. Lubrication of components for GSAT-1 and INSAT-3B is now in progress.

Liquid propulsion

Completion of qualification tests on GSLV liquid propulsion stage, L-40, and its propellant mock-up trials at SHAR Centre as well as realisation of liquid propulsion stages, PS-2 and PS-4 for PSLV-C2 'and PS-1 control systems including injection valves and SITVC systems have been the major accomplishments under liquid propulsion area during the year.

In the cryogenic upper stage project, thrust chamber of 12 tonne cryogenic engine has undergone hot test under derated condition.

The performance of second stage of PSLV during PSLV-C1 flight has been analysed and simulations carried out to pinpoint the anomaly that occurred in the 4th stage of PSLV-C1. PS-4 stage for the PSLV-C2 has been integrated and for the strapon stage of PSLV-C2, SITVC tank assemblies have been realised. The first stage reaction control system PS-1 RCS have also been integrated.

The L-40 stage of GSLV has been realised for ground resonance test. All the four strap-on stages for the first developmental flight of GSLV is under fabrication while the second stage is in the final stages of integration and testing. The SITVC packages for the first GSLV flight have undergone qualifications.

For the satellites, bi-propellant system for INSAT-2E has been fully realised. The system has also been realised for INSAT-3B which uses indigenously fabricated propulsion tanks. Integration of propellant systems of GSAT-1 to be launched onboard GSLV-D1, is under progress. In this satellite, a 10 N bi-propellant engine is being used.

Configuration of INSAT-3A propulsion system has been finalised and hardware fabrication initiated.

For IRS-P4, fabrication of a majority of components including surface tension tanks, hydrazine thrusters, valves, transducers, etc., has been completed. Detailed design of the propulsion system for IRS-P5 has been completed and fabrication initiated.

Research and development work have continued towards improving injectors, optimisation of regeneratively cooled cryo engines, improvement in ignitors of cryo stage, etc.

Mechanical engineering

Mechanical engineering activities during the year were mainly directed towards realisation of hardware for PSLV, GSLV, Rohini sounding rockets, IRS and INSAT spacecraft.

In the area of launch vehicle mechanisms, stage auxiliary systems for PSLV-C2 have been realised. Functional qualification tests on the separation systems of KITSAT and TUBSAT have been completed. For GSLV, launcher hold and release system has undergone functional testing on the launch pedestal with simulated vehicle interface. Strap-on assembly for propellant mock up test has also been completed. GS-1 system level test with two plane separation has been completed. Payload adaptor and stub adaptor have been fabricated and full scale heatshield separation/jettisoning test was completed. Satellite separation system and GS2/CS separation system have been realised. One set of cryogenic stage separation systems simulator assembly was fabricated during the year.

Technology developments in the areas of shape memory alloy for active damping, adaptive material for smart structures, 4 m diameter heatshield for future GSLV, grooved band joint, multiple satellite launch adaptor, APS acoustic protection system based on Helmholtz resonator, deboost motors for payload recovery, etc. have continued during the year.

Mechanical fabrication of various spacecraft elements for INSAT-2E, IRS-P4, GSAT-1 and INSAT-3B have been completed. In the area of spacecraft mechanisms, fabrication of nut type canister and transition guide for a flexible solar array boom is in progress. Assembly of boom elements for a verification model of an articulated lattice boom has been initiated. Fabrication of all mechanism components for Synthetic Aperture Radar (SAR) antenna has been completed and waveguide panel assembled during the year.

Demonstration model of an antenna pointing drive mechanism has been assembled and tested. Characterisation of shape memory alloy actuators using direct heating methods has been made. Detailed design of mechanism of an unfurlable antenna has been completed during the year.

In Robotics, assembly of shoulder joints, elbow joint and three degree of freedom wrist mechanism has been completed during the year. Trials have been carried out on a simulated joint to verify motor control software, electronic hardware and trajectory software at joint level.

Mission planning and analysis

Spacecraft health monitoring, analysis and control software for INSAT-2E has been developed and tests are in progress. A new programme has been developed to carry out auto-commanding of INSAT-2C, whenever momentum/re action wheel-off is detected. The flight dynamic system software for INSAT-2E has been implemented on the mission computer and first level test and evaluation completed during the year. Mission analysis activities including apogee manoeuvre strategy, colocation of INSAT-3A with 2B and 2C, have been carried out. Analysis for GSAT has also been carried out. GSAT mission planning is in progress.

Design and development software to automate activities, multi-mission front-end interface and payload specific operations of IRS-P4 has been completed. A quick look browse software for IRS-1C and IRS-11) has been developed and implemented at IRS data receiving stations at Norman, USA and Japan.

Preliminary Design Review of mission plan and analysis for the ground segment of IRS-P4 has been completed. Development of spacecraft simulator for all relevant subsystems is in progress.

Power

A number of flexible substrate combinations have been fabricated towards developing a flexible solar panels.

Thermal tests with solar cells bonded on to the coupons have been completed.

In power control electronics design of a mother board package common to IRS and INSAT series of satellites is progressing. Development and qualification of Hybrid Micro Circuit (HMC) version of DC/DC converter regulator for spacecraft applications and a PC based automatic test equipment for the same and a modularised, linear solar array simulator are the other activities.

Propellants, polymers, chemicals and materials and composites

Development of low aluminium HTPB propellant has been completed during the year. In the Polymers and Chemicals area, development of new products is continuing and during the year six items have been cleared for qualification and eleven items are under pre-qualification tests. Different types of adhesives have been produced for PSLV-C2 flight and 553 different types of vibration isolators realised for use in C-band coherent Transponder for GSLV has been qualified. An external encapsulation with modified epoxy for isolation/ shielding has been developed for high-frequency slip ring assembly.

Production of various chemicals like HTPB, potting compounds, prepolymers, light weight foam mandrels, vibration damping blocks, cowling cones/nozzle caps for retro and ullage motors, hydrazine, MON-3 and paints required by launch vehicles and satellites continued during the year.

Silver-Zinc cells for sounding rockets and GSLV project and nickel-cadmium cells for IRS-P5 have also been realised. Processing technology for hydrogen electrodes using platinum catalyst has been carried out

In the materials area, silver-graphite brush blocks

for Doppler Weather Radar slip ring assembly have been realised. Double layered turbine seal rings for cryogenic engine application, somarium-cobalt magnets for latch valves and reaction control thrusters and RF switches have been produced. Scale up experiments for converting low modulus pitch based carbon fibres to high modulus variety have been conducted. Forging and rolling studies of aluminium alloy-silicon-carbon particulate composites have been conducted. A number of magnesium alloy castings for PSLV, GSLV and INSAT have been developed. Raw materials such as rings, plates and filler wires, gas bottles have been fabricated. Chemical, physical and spectroscopic analysis and metallographical characterisation have been continued during the year.

In the area of composites, nozzles, throat inserts, igniter cases, motor cases for PSLV solid propulsion stages and composite payload adaptor have been realised during the year. Nozzle throat insert for GSLV-D1 flight has also been realised.

A high performance motor case for effecting weight reduction in the present PSLV third stage motor case has been developed and it has undergone burst pressure test.

Composites elements of solar panels, yokes antennas, solar array drive cone, solar flaps, pressurant tanks for INSAT-2E, INSAT-3B and GSAT-1 have been realised during the year.

Development of solar panel using reticulation process with carbon fabric and aluminium honeycomb core is in progress. Flight unit of IRS-P4 MSMR payload composite elements and Ku-band antenna made of aluminium-CFRP honeycomb, titanium lined pressurant tanks, etc., for INSAT-3B have also been realised during the year.

Satellite communications

Technology development activities under satellite communications were mainly directed towards INSAT-3 series of satellites during the year. Design of all three shaped reflectors for C-band extended coverage , extended C-band Indian coverage and the Ku-band Indian coverage and their respective feeds for INSAT-3A have been completed. Fabrication and testing of INSAT-313 communication payloads is in an advanced stage with most of the units having undergone test and evaluation. 0.6 m diameter Ku-band antenna and Ku-band mux/demux have also undergone test and evaluation. For GSAT, most of the subsystems are in advanced stage of fabrication and testing and test and evaluation on CxS receivers, S-band mux filter and S-band driver amplifier have already been completed.

After test and evaluation, redundant hub equipment for INSAT-MSS reporting system has been installed. Development of multi-carrier (4 carriers) hub electronics has been taken up for operations with up to 600 reporting terminals. More reliable, flexible and compact size DSP- based Burst Demodulator and NCO-based tunable down converter has been developed and tested with satellite.

Under GSAT-1 applications project, it is planned to demonstrate Digital Sound, Data and TV Broadcast in S-band. Under the Digital Sound and Data Broadcasting (DSDB) service, it is planned to multiplex 15 channels of audio and data and transmit them in a 256 kbps data stream through a VSAT like up-link. Hybrid Internet service is planned to be demonstrated using in small S-band receiver to down load large volume data for short duration. Transmission of compressed Digital TV at 2 Mbps in multi-channel mode and multi-carrier mode is also planned to be demonstrated with small S-band receive antenna. During the year, development of components for Hybrid Internet Service has started. Extensive interaction and concept demonstration of DSDB to potential user like AIR, IMD, IGNOU, PTI, etc., have also been carried out.

As part of JDCP network operations, a 4.5 m diameter vehicle mounted VSAT terminal with associated uplink equipment has been installed in Bhopal for conducting JDCP talk-back programmes. A software has been developed for the DAMA system by which data broadcasting facility has been introduced between the teaching end and interactive classrooms at 12 blocks of Jhabua district. A 64 kbps digital talk-back system has been designed and successfully tested, with satellite.

A multimedia data dissemination system for multimedia applications like distance education, dissemination of meteorological data, digital talkback, etc., has been designed. Development of variable bit rate DSP based BPSK demodulator operating from 1200 bps to 64 kbps has been completed. System concept of Digital Cyclone Warning Dissemination System has also been demonstrated.

Safety

Space programme, in spite of involving use of cryogenic fluids, liquid and solid propellants and pyrotechnic materials, continued to be free from any major accidents during the year. Safety groups set up at various Space Centres continued to provide guidance on safety aspects during design and construction of facilities and their locations. During the year such assistance was provided for the establishment of second launch pad at SHAR Centre, production of solid propellant motors and servicing of liquid propellant to liquid engines, realisation of pyrotechnic and test and evaluation of rocket motors.

Major tests on L-40 liquid propulsion stage of GSLV, developmental tests on C-12 cryogenic engine thrust chamber and acceptance tests on PSLV - fourth stage, liquid apogee motor and reaction control thrusters of spacecraft have been carried out without any accident. Detailed safety study of the cryogenic fluid circuits in the cryogenic main engine and stage test stand has been completed and safety recommendations taken up for implementation. Safety and fire protection systems required for carrying out commissioning trials in test stand have been commissioned. The cryogenic main engine and stage test facilities have also been commissioned under required safety standards and procedures. The storage facilities for earth storable propellants have been reviewed during the year and safety recommendations are being implemented. Necessary safety surveillance in fabrication and testing of INSAT-2E and GSAT for pressure test, vibration test etc., has been made. MCF and ISTRAC took necessary precaution in ensuring personnel safety in relation to radiation hazardous, etc. Safety support extended for effluent treatment, propellant disposal, pressure testing, etc.

ISRO safety office coordinated safety audit, recruitment of fire personnel, organising inter centre workshops and interaction with statutory bodies.

Safety inspections, audits, surprise checks and drill on various hazardous areas, electrical installations, laboratory activities, operational facilities in Space Centre have continued. Safety awareness and promotional activities have continued through observation of national safety day, fire service day, issue of safety posters, screening of safety films, organizing in plant safety training programme, etc.

Solid propulsion

The solid propulsion motor of RH-300 sounding rocket has been redesigned to meet extreme operating temperature conditions. Thermal performance data in terms of erosion rate and heat of ablation has been generated through ablative tests. Grain designs for S-200 motor, RH-300 motor for low-temperature applications and a primary solid motor for airbreathing flight demonstrator has also been completed.

Production of ammonium perchlorate and strontium perchlorate and various types of other solid propellant constituents has continued to meet the needs of PSLV-C2 and sounding rockets.

Pyros for PSLV-C2 and RH-560 flight have been realised. Pyro valves, cable-cutters and bolt cutters for INSAT-2E, INSAT-3B, IRS-P4 have also been realised during the year.

Spacecraft integration

A new QPSK demodulator has been developed for INSAT-VHRR checkout system. A multichannel excitation unit has been developed for simultaneous excitation of up to 12 channels of communication payloads with standard C-band transponder configurations. Solar array simulators for INSAT-2E has been fabricated and a battery simulator fabrication is in progress.

Structures

Structural design and analysis of 4 m diameter CFRP heat-shield and payload adaptor of GSLV equipment bay and payload structure of PSLV have been carried out during the year. Structural analysis of high performance third stage motor case of PSLV and CFRP support structure for multi-frequency satellite microwave radiometer of IRS-P4 payload has been completed. Modified fin design for RH-560 Mk-H sounding rocket has been completed. Acoustic emission tests have been carried out for titanium-lined kevlar epoxy pressure vessels.

A video imaging and processing technique has been developed for remote measurement and recordings during structural qualification tests of certain GSLV structures. Ground Resonance Test (GRT) for GSLV has been completed. Dynamic characteristics for the entire flight duration of PSLV-C2 using lateral, longitudinal and torsional modes have been studied.

Further improvements have been incorporated in structural design and analysis software, FEAST-C, FEAST-NL, PREWIN, etc.

Design studies on Carbon Fibre Reinforced Plastic (CFRP) main structure for spacecraft have been carried out. A technique has been developed to predict the frequency of non-uniform panels to acoustic excitation using statistical energy analysis.

Systems reliability

Vikram Sarabhai Space Centre, under Thiruvananthapuram, has been certified under ISO-9000 during the year. Efforts are continuing for implementing procedures related to ISO-9000 for hardware and software developed by various ISRO Centres. Strict adherence to quality protocols and implementation of quality assurance and quality control procedures have continued towards ensuring realisation of systems and subsystems for the launch vehicle and spacecraft projects.

Quality assurance aspects have been kept in view during subsystem and system level testing, integrated spacecraft testing, checkout and integration of INSAT-2E and IRS-P4 spacecraft. Quality monitoring activities pertaining to launch complex preparation and propellant processing activities, facility readiness during the test and evaluation, instrumentation systems at liquid propellant and storage complexes.

Test and evaluation of flight and stand-by packages for PSLV-C2 and flight units of GSLV-D1 have been carried out during the year. Test and evaluation of flight and stand-by packages for RH-560 Mk-II sounding rocket were also carried out. Reliability analysis of subsystems of INSAT-2E, IRS-P4, PSLV-C2 and GSLV-D1 using failure mode effects and criticality analysis, reliability apportionment and fault-tree analysis, has been carried out. About four lakh electronic parts, including a large number of Very Large Scale Integrated devices, were screened for use on board satellites and launch vehicles.

Training of personnel have been undertaken by the soldering school on high reliability interconnection and fabrication techniques.

QA aspects have been kept in view in the programme of development of space components and materials in the fabrication of hardware at external work centres has also been provided. Quality control procedures have been drawn up for the miniaturisation.

Telemetry, Tracking and Command (TTC)

Under INSAT TTC operations, ground systems at INSAT Master Control Facility (MCF) have been augmented for INSAT-213, keeping in view the transponders in lower extended C-band frequency and the VHRR/CCD cameras that this satellite carries. The feed of Satellite Control Earth Stations (SCES-5) has been modified for wide frequency range for Ku-band operations with 7.2 m diameter limited motion antenna. A sixth earth station (SCES-6) is being added for INSAT-2E and INSAT-3 series of satellites. SCES-6 will have a full motion antenna with 92/11m diameter. Limited motion antennas of 7.2 m diameter are also being added at SCES -1, 2 and 4.

MCF supported during the year, four on-orbit satellite operations, (INSAT-1D, 2A, 2B, 2C). Detailed characterisation of INSAT-2DT satellite acquired from

ARABSAT was carried out. Electronics and processing systems have been added for TTC operation of INSAT-2DT. Seven transponders of THAICOM-3 satellite have also been characterised. MCF provided inorbit test support for the US PAS-7 satellite of PanAmSat Corporation.

TTC support to low earth orbit satellites, IRS-1A, IRS-113, IRS-1C, IRS-113, IRS-P2, IRS-P3 and SROSS-C2 spacecraft, has continued from ISRO Telemetry, Tracking and Command Network. Control and monitoring of these satellites is being carried out in a multi-satellite environment. A satellite communication network has been established for supporting IRS and SROSS mission operations between spacecraft control Centre and ground stations at Bangalore, Lucknow, Shadnagar, SHAR, Mauritius, Bearslake and German Space Operations Centre, Germany. TTC interfaces for the forthcoming satellites IRS-P4, IRS-P5 and IRS-P6 including planning of communication and computer requirements are being worked out.

Augmentation of SHAR-2 and Port Blair TTC ground stations has been completed. TTC station at Biak in Indonesia has been established and qualification tests are in progress. Brunei station system integration to support GSLV mission has been completed and the station is planned to be commissioned by April 1999. Interface details with PSLV and GSLV for planning TTC support requirements have been worked out.

SHAR, Thiruvananthapuram and Port Blair ground stations also supported RH-560 Mk-II launched from Sriharikota during the year. Besides, TTC support was also provided to EUTELSAT mission.

Research and development activities have continued. Development of a multi-function receiver and range and range-rate system has been initiated. Two ranging systems are being fabricated for ISTRAC TTC stations. A digital servo system has been developed for use in the TTC stations. Fabrication of subsystems for the Doppler Weather Radar for India Meteorological Department is in an advanced stage and the first radar is expected to be commissioned in 1999.

A SPACENET with nodes at ISAC, ISRO HQ, SHAR, SAC, VSSC, Shadnagar, Balanagar and MCF with the hub located at ISTRAC, Bangalore has been established during the year for voice, data and video conferencing.

Detailed risk assessment for Indian satellites from the Leonid meteorides had been made and plans worked out and implemented during the storm in November 1998. No damage occurred to any of the satellites.

Thermal

Thermal protection data updates for PSLV-C2 has been completed during the year. Thermal analysis of various components housed in GSLV strap-on (L-40) base shroud has been completed using both theoretical methods and experimental data. Solar heating of cryogenic upper stage has been estimated for various pre-launch and flight phases. Qualification of thermal protection system on RH-560 Mk-II sustainer fins has been the other activity during the year.

Sub-scale tests for determining the base heating in GSLV due to plume interaction have also been completed. Thermal and mechanical design of thermal boot for L-40 stage of GSLV has been made and demonstrated through static test.

In the spacecraft area, development of a split-stirling cryo-refrigerator having flexure bearing has continued for GSAT A study on power, size and weight of a charcoal-nitrogen system hydride cooler has continued and trials have been conducted to study packing efficiency. Trials have been conducted on white anodizing on aluminium alloys by adding ammonium molybdate additive and checked for optical properties. The process of silver plating on aluminium components has been qualified during the year.

A heat-pipe radiator panel for GSAT-1 spacecraft has been realised. As part of large size heat-pipe radiator development, trials have been carried out on bending the heat-pipe envelope to required angle.

During the year, Redundant Strapdown Inertial Navigation System (RESINS) and Rate Gyro Package (RGP) for PSLV-C2/IRS-P4 Mission, simulation and proto model of RESINS and RGP and new checkout units for GSLV and inertial components for INSAT-2E and INSAT-3B have been realised. 3-Axis RGPs have been realised for PSLV-C2 and GSLV simulation purpose, during the year.

5

Space Sciences

Space Science research under Indian space programme is mainly carried out at Physical Research Laboratory,(PRL), Ahmedabad, Space Physics Laboratory (SPL), Thiruvananthapuram and ISRO Satellite Centre, Bangalore. The National Mesosphere-Stratosphere-Troposphere Radar Facility (NMRF), near Tirupati, which is an autonomous society established and funded by the DOS, is available for atmospheric research by scientists from universities and research institutions. Space science research is also supported in several universities and research institutions under Sponsored Research Programme of DOS.

Physical Research Laboratory (PRL), Ahmedabad

PRL is an autonomous institution supported mainly by DOS. The research activities carried out in PRL relate to four main disciplines: Astronomy and Astrophysics, Planetary Atmospheres and Aeronomy, Earth Sciences and Solar System Studies and Theoretical Physics. The laboratory has also added to its research programme, the nonlinear dynamics and computational sciences and laser physics and quantum optics. PRL has a strong graduate programme leading to Ph.D. degree. It also offers opportunities for carrying out postdoctoral research.

Astronomy and astrophysics

Coordinated observations have been carried out using the 1.2 m diameter optical telescope and in the gamma-ray region using gamma-ray telescope facility at Mt. Abu to study the variability behaviour of blazars Mrk 421 and Mrk 501. Burst activity was detected simultaneously in optical polarisation and gamma ray flux in Mrk 501. This is an important finding to put constraints on the existing models of blazars. Mrk 421 also shows increased activity in gamma rays and optical polarisation. A systematic study of a sample of star burst galaxies has been carried out to study the morphology and to locate the star forming regions in such galaxies. Optical and near infrared imaging observations have been conducted using the 1.2 m diameter telescope at Gurushikhar, Mt. Abu. A variety of morphological types have been found to host the star burst phenomenon. Regions of intense star formation, away from the nuclear region, have been detected in several cases.

Age of the burst, based on model fitting, was found between one to ten million years. Study of kinematics of Planetary Nebula is continuing. Fabry-Perot observations on planetary nebula NGC 246 in [OIII] 5007A line has demonstrated interaction of this planetary nebula with ISM. This is for the first time that such interaction of ISM and PN have been detected experimentally. A lunar occultation of the bright Mira variable R Leo was observed at Gurushikhar observatory on December 18,1997. The event was observed at a wavelength of 3.36 micron with a bandwidth of 0.05 micron. A detailed analysis of the occultation fight curve has resulted in a uniform disk angular size of 35 _ 4 milli arc sec. A subsequent occultation of R Leo in March 1998 was recorded from Calar-Alto Observatory (Spain) in K-band (2.2 micron). Since the 82 days separation between the two events is a significant fraction of the 313 day period of the variability of R Leo, a detectable variation in angular size is expected and is being investigated.

Planetary atmospheres and aeronomy

The Backscatter Lidar at Mt. Abu has been augmented to measure Raman scattered radiation from nitrogen molecules. This has enabled obtaining atmospheric density and temperature information in the troposphere and lower stratosphere which is not possible from Rayleigh scattering measurements because of interference from aerosol scattering. The Lidar is now operated both in Raman mode and Rayleigh mode to obtain air density and temperature profiles continuously from troposphere to mesosphere. Mie scattering measurements show that the stratosphere is void of any volcanic aerosol layer. After major eruption by Pinatubo in 1991, whose effect subsided in early 1995, no appreciable effect of any volcano in the stratosphere has been seen since 1995. As part of Indian Ocean Experiment (INDOEX), spatial and temporal variations in aerosol characteristics have been studied over the Arabian Sea and the tropical Indian Ocean during cruise conducted during February-March 1998. For the first time, continuous data sets have been obtained both at north and south of the Inter Tropical Convergence Zone (ITCZ). Particles of size less than 0.2 micrometre size have been found transported to thousands of kilometre from the continents. Extensive measurements of Ozone, CO, NO, etc., have been made. The air samples collected have been analysed for CH4, SF6, etc. For the first time, measurements of these gases have been made across the ITCZ which separates the pristine clean Indian Ocean in the South with the polluted region in the North. Lower ozone (5-10 ppb) in the southern part of ITCZ has been observed compared to north of ITCZ (15-20 ppb). The second field phase of INDOEX has started on January 20,1999. Data from MST radar collected during January-February 1996 has been analysed and the vertical wind velocity has been found to be below the detection limit. Horizontal wind vector is found to rotate from north to south and then from south to north via east in the altitude region of 5-18 km. Analysis shows that this is due to the rotation of the mean wind. Also it appears that this rotation is not by equatorial Kelvin wave, predominant at the tropics. Rotation of horizontal wind vector is clearly discernible.

While production of ionisation in the stratosphere is supposed to be due to cosmic rays and the intensity of the cosmic rays is supposed to vary inversely with solar activity, resulting in higher ion conductivity during low solar activity and vice versa, balloon-borne measurements of conductivity over Hyderabad have shown a direct correlation with solar activity. Further investigation of this mechanism is being undertaken.

Rocket measurements over Thumba and Sriharikota have indicated almost similar features, both in magnitude and direction, in the E-region primary east-west electric field observed at the equator and off-the-equator. But the vertical electric field has been found to be much stronger over the equator.

A balloon flight has been successfully conducted from the TIFR Balloon Launch Facility at Hyderabad on April 18,1998 to collect air samples in the 6 to 37 kin altitude. The air samples are being analysed.

The technique of estimating mesopause temperatures during day-time conditions using ground based optical techniques, which had been validated earlier by using simultaneous satellite measurements, have been successfully used in retrieving this important parameter from a low latitude station, Kolhapur and large scale, hitherto unknown, variabilities gleaned for the first time.

The magnetospheric space as well as weather related processes and the eventual high-latitude low-latitude coupling effects like Equatorial Temperature and Wind Anomaly have been parameterised using geomagnetic Dst index and ionospheric thermospheric conditions. This enables the model to reproduce observed variabilities.

Using a non-linear numerical simulation model, the mechanism for suppressing large scale plasma plume events has been identified. Development of long wavelength plasma plume events can be confined to bottom of the ionosphere in a localised region with the combined effects of shears in the zonal plasma flow and a night time westward electric field. The variabilities in the occurrence characteristic are shown to depend on the variabilities in the pre-reversal enhancement in the zonal electric field. The ionisation hole experiment conducted using sounding rockets has revealed the presence of molecular ions till about 300 kin height confirming the earlier measurements. Linear analysis of Rayleigh-Taylor instability, which is believed to be primary causative mechanism in the presence of double-ion species, has revealed that the growth rate depends on the number densities of both the ion species. This is in contrast to single ionic constituent wherein the growth rate is independent of number density. The numerical calculation under realistic situation has revealed that the growth rate of instability reduces with the introduction of second dominant (NO +) ions and never exceeds the growth rate corresponding to single ionic constituent.

Analysis of data collected from electric field and electron density probes carried on board a sounding rocket has indicated that the vertical electric field fluctuations are co-located with electron density fluctuations, the spectrum of electric field fluctuations in the vertical direction over the intermediate, transitional and short ranges has been given for the first time and large-scale structures are located essentially at same altitudes during the ascent and the descent of the rocket. Also, the unique feature of this profile is the observation of irregularities with vertical scale sizes upto about 6 km in 160-250 kin region. Based on the scale sizes of these structures, it has been suggested that gravity waves could be responsible for their generation. The estimation of effective growth rate of irregularities generated through Generalised Rayleigh-Taylor Instability (GRTI) above 200 km has been made and it is found that the growth rate (g) is positive only when L is negative suggesting that electric field and vertical winds contribute more than gravitational term in the production of irregularities above 200 km.

Observations of CI 1931A emission in ultraviolet spectra of comets have shown that a large fraction of carbon atoms in the cometary coma are produced in the metastable 1D excited state. A coupled chemistry-transport model has been used to study the chemistry of C (1D) atom and the mechanisms for the production of CI 1931A in the near nucleus environment. Dissociation of CO by solar UV photon and photoelectron impact are the dominant mechanisms of the C (1D) production in the cometary coma. The CI 1931A emission is found to be governed dominantly by density distribution of CO and C (1D). CI 1931A emission brightness is predicted on comet 46P/Wirtanen, the target of ROSETTA space mission.

The fluorescence excitation spectra of NO 2 have been studied and life times measured at the excitation photon wavelength 390-490 nm at an interval of 0.2 nm using an excimer laser pumped tunable dye laser as photon source.

Earth science and solar system studies

Simultaneous photospheric, chromospheric and magnetic

field data have been obtained using video magnetograph at Udaipur Solar Observatory (USO) to study magnetic field evolution in some active regions in the ascending phase of Cycle 23. Large gradients, flux imbalance and motions of about 4 - 0.8 km/s, flux variations upto 1013 Mx/s and new flux emergence are some important features of flaring areas. Solar activity and synoptic observation for solar flares and active region physics has continued. H-alpha intensity oscillations have been detected in two solar flares which occurred on November 15,1989 and April 20,1991. Analysis of relative intensity variation has showed prominent 5- and 3- min modes.

Investigation of possible systematic errors in determining solar radius from f-mode frequencies, which are largely localised just below the surface, has been made. It is inferred that input physics governing the structure of outermost layers of the Sun has significant influence on the estimated radius. The best estimate of solar radius is 695.77+0.1 mega-metre.

Using p-mode frequencies obtained from the GONG network for the period August 23,1995 to August 16,1996, it has been shown that frequency shifts are very sensitive to structural changes due to solar activity cycle. Study of p-modes and their scattering properties with reference to its amplitude and frequency in the active and emerging flux regions is being carried out to understand the interaction of p-modes with magnetic activity.

It has been deduced from the analysis of carbon isotopes in soils of Permian geological era (280 million years ago) obtained from Central India that the atmospheric CO2 level was about 8 times higher than present. Intensity of monsoon rainfall for the past 3500 years over Central India has been estimated from isotopic analysis of speleothem, a cave calote deposit. The total variation during this period is within 20 percent. Geochemical studies on climatic condition in Nal Sarovar region of Gujarat indicate a high rainfall regime about 50,000 years ago as indicated by the presence of a red bed of clay. Thermoluminescence and optically-stimulated luminescence dating of fine sands from Thar desert region indicates three different climatic phases during the past 66,000 years: an and phase during 66 to 60 ka, normal rainfall period during 60 to 25 ka, and an and phase during 25 to 10 ka.

Although evidence for 26AI has been found in some of the very early solar system solids, its presence in samples of meteorites that are distinct products of crystallisation from a melt have not been demonstrated yet. First evidence for the presence of 26AI in such a meteorite has been found through ion microprobe studies of Al-Mg isotopic, compositions in samples of the Piplia-Kalan meteorite, which fell in Rajasthan in 1996. The evidence suggest 26AI as a heat source for melting of planetesimals in the early solar system.

Mantle-derived samples like diamonds, mid-ocean ridge basalt glasses and ultramafic xenoliths as probes for the Earth's mantle have been analysed and found that the nitrogen isotopic composition (15N/14N) is depleted in the pristine mantle by about 1.5 percent, relative to earths atmosphere. Analysis of two meteorites, Shergotty and ALH84001, that are believed to be fragment of Mars, shows that nitrogen isotopic composition of Mars is also depleted by about 4 percent relative to terrestrial atmospheric value. Thus, both the mantles of Earth and Mars seem to have a light nitrogen isotopic signature and suggest that the building blocks of these planets could be enstatite chondrite material that are characterised by light nitrogen isotopic compositions. Three stony meteorites, Piplia-Kalan, Didwana and Lohawat, that fell in Rajasthan during 1992-96, have been analysed for their mineralogical and chemical characteristics and have been classified as eucrite, enstatite and howardite type respectively. Detailed studies of the Piplia-Kalan eucrite indicate it to be one of the oldest eucrite, making it a good candidate for looking for records of very early solar system processes that led to formation of eucrites which are product of melt crystallisation on asteroidal sized objects.

Ages of several dykes of Deccan Province have been determined using Ar-Ar dating technique to complement geochronological data obtained from the lava flows. Of the ten dyke samples dated, three yielded well-defined plateau ages while others showed late disturbances in Ar isotopic systematics. The three ages obtained are, 70.7 _ 0.8 Ma, 65.4 _ 0.7 Ma and 66.6 _ 4.6 Ma, which span the same range of ages as those of lava flows. These results reinforce earlier findings that Deccan volcanism had an extended duration beginning at about 70 Ma and lasting upto 63 Ma.

Ages of carbonatite rocks found in western India in close association with Deccan basalts have been determined using Ar-Ar dating technique. The ages of the carbonatites are found to be about 65 million years coincident with the Cretaceous Tertiary boundary (KTB) extinction event. The emplacement of carbonatites during KTB event could have released large amount of CO2 and SO2 into the earth's atmosphere that may have added additional stress and accelerated the process that led to extinction of species at this geologic boundary. It is found that concentrations of iridium measured in basalt samples from Anjar, Kutchch (Gujarat), associated with Deccan volcanism range from a few to hundred picogram-V gram suggesting that contribution of iridium from Deccan volcanism to the global budget of iridium at KTB layer is less than 10 percent. The source of iridium enrichment in KTB is thus extraterrestrial in nature and support an asteroidal/ cometary impact.

The Rhenium-Osmium (Re-0s) dating method has been applied to obtain the age and isotopic composition of osmium. in black-shale of Himalaya. The age is found to be about 600 million years for black-shale. The osmium isotopic ratio (187Re/186Os) in them is much higher than the crustal value of 10, suggesting that black-shale could be a significant source of radiogenic osmium in the rivers draining the Himalaya and hence for the steady increase in osmium isotopic ratio (187Re/186Os) in the world oceans over the last forty million years.

Theoretical physics

A compact formula of the form factor containing one Jacobi polynomial for transition between arbitrary circular states has been derived. Analytical properties of the form factor, such as location of real zeros or its symptotic expression for large principal quantum numbers, are essentially determined by known behaviour of Jacobi polynomial. For optically allowed transition between circular states, the form factor reduces to a simple expression containing associated Legendre polynomial, The formula obtained can also be used for numerical work.

Implications of the discovery ot a non-zero neutrino mass at Superkamioka Laboratory in Japan on the standard theory of elementary particles has been analysed. The results hint at very mildly broken Le-Lt-Lm symmetry. Schemes, have been proposed to explain all the available experimental nutrino masses. Implications of an experimental discovery at DESY in Hamburg of a new particle "leptoquark", which carries lepton as well as baryon numbers, on supersymmetric theory have been examined. It is suggested that modifications are needed in the minimal and commonly accepted version of supersymmetric theory in order that it accommodated leptoquarks. In an ongoing study of possible signatures of CP violation in accelerator-based physics, possible ways for finding chromo-electric dipole moment of top quark have been suggested.

Study of group theoretical models of structure of heavy nuclei near proton drip line is continuing. A model, based on Wigner's SU(4) symmetry for generating new coupling schemes for heavy N = Z odd nuclei near the proton drip line, has been developed and spectra and characteristics of g-ray electric quadrupole. transitions of N = Z nuclei has been predicted.

Investigation of Jupiter's magnetosphere interaction with Io-plasma torus has shown that the effect of mass-loading near Io-satellite generates an enhanced current density in the shear region which produces a high level of kinetic Alfven waves for particle acceleration and this can generate various emissions as observed in that region.

The external and internal structures of the magnetic field of a slowly rotating neutron star having matter with different equations of state have been analysed. It has been found that the increase in the field strength from surface to core is quite large (upto 30 percent) in rotating case as compared to the non-rotating case. In the studies related to numerical relativity, the cactus code has been used to study the evolution of a system consisting of a Schwarzschild black and Brill type gravitational wave, in which the outgoing modes have been found to be predominantly quasi-normal modes.

The work on the quantum wave functions of two dimensional classically chaotic coupled quartic oscillator system has continued with studies made on both classical and quantum aspects of the problem. The subclass of channel localised states reported earlier have been found to be exponentially localised in unperturbed basis. Following earlier work on classical stability oscillations of isolated short-time periodic orbits, called channel orbits which scar such states, it has been established that information entropy of channel localised states is strongly correlated to these classical stability oscillations. The minimum entropic states are obtained at parameter values for which the channel orbit is about to undergo a pitchfork bifurcation.

The method for determination of parameters of a complex system from time series data using a combination of adaptive control and synchronisation has been developed. This method introduces a new concept of dynamic minimisation of the synchronisation error. The method is shown to work even when the unknown parameter appears in the evolution equations of variables other than the one for which the time, series is given.

In the field of quantum optics and laser physics, extensive research have been made in the areas of coherent control of optical processes, quantum state engineering, wave packet dynamics and near field optics. It is shown that the tendency of a laser beam to break into a filamentary structure in passing through a non-linear optical medium can be largely suppressed by proper tailoring of the vacuum field that interacts with the laser beam. In another application of coherent control, a coherent coupling, between the intermediate level of a cascade system (in its excited state) with a fourth level, creates coherence in cascade emission. As a result, quantum beats in correlations between the two spontaneously emitted photons have been observed. It is also shown that the coupling makes dipole matrix elements non-orthogonal, which is the prime requirement for creating atomic coherences by spontaneous emission.

A scheme to reconstruct a two-mode entangled state in cavity QED has been suggested by using interaction of a V-configuration three-level atom and by driving the cavity field. The probability of atom being in its initial ground state yields two-mode Wigner characteristic function, the processing of which gives density matrix elements.

Research is continuing in wave packet dynamics. It has been found, both analytically and numerically, that as in the case of harmonic oscillator coherent states, SU(1,1), coherent states also revive (fully and fractionally) under the action of a two-mode generic Hamiltonian. However, in the present case, revival features depend crucially on difference in photon numbers of the two modes. These revival phenomena are vulnerable to perturbations in realistic situations. For example, it has been shown that the revival pattern in wave packet dynamics of a particle confined to a finite square well will be affected by tunnelling effects, a whole range of revivals and super- revivals will be allowed and the revival times will depend on the depth of the well. Sub-wavelength resolution using evanescent waves in both incident and scattered waves has been demonstrated. A theoretical framework has been developed to show how the radiation from a dipole near a structure serves as its probe.

Space Physics Laboratory (SPL), Thiruvananthapuram

SPL conducts research mainly on atmospheric aerosols, boundary layers physics, atmospheric dynamics, ionospheric-magnetosphere. During the year, a comprehensive analytical model has been developed to describe the altitude structure of aerosol number density in the mixing region. The seasonal pattern of surface aerosol flux obtained from this model has shown two distinct peaks - one in winter and the other during south-west monsoon months. The long term data on Columnar Aerosol Optical Depth (CAOD) from Multi Wavelength Radiometer (MWR) and mixing region Aerosol Optical Depth (AOD) from CW Lidar have been analysed and at it shows a systematic long-term increasing trend in AOD, the mixing region and also in troposphere at Thiruvananthapuram since 1989.

Mass loading and size distribution of near surface aerosols have also been studied. The climatology of AOD over Indian subcontinent has been established using data from a network of MWR at Thiruvananthapuram, Mysore, Visakhapatnam, Minicoy and Mauritius. The network is being augmented by addition of stations at Jodhpur, Anantpur and Dibrugarh.

Subsoil temperature data is being collected regularly at Thumba, Kariavattom and Lucknow from which soil surface temperature and soil diffusivity are derived. Advanced Regional Prediction System (ARPS) which is a 3D, non-hydrostatic numerical mesoscale model, has been installed with graphic support.

The horizontal winds measured by Mesosphere Stratosphere and Troposphere (MST) radar for three diurnal cycles spread over September-December 1995 have been analysed to bring out the diurnal tidal characteristics in the troposphere - lower stratospheric region. The analysis of radar data during vernal equinox, summer and winter seasons is in progress. A method has been developed to estimate vertical flux of zonal momentum of this equatorial Kelvin and Rossby Gravity (RG) waves from MST data. A Monte Carlo model has been developed to describe the degradation of low energy electrons in SO2 gas to study the photoelectron impact ionisation and excitation in the Io's atmosphere which gives the Analytical Yield Spectra. It has been shown that the line of sight drift velocity of 3 m scale irregularities observed with MST radar in the attitude of range 90-97 km corresponds to the meridional component of the neutral wind.

Development of a High Frequency (HF) radar operating at 18 MHz and 9 MHz with a peak power of 50 kW, has been completed. Integration of all subsystems of Multi Wavelength Lidar (MWL) system has also been completed. Trial operation has also been conducted and test data upto an altitude of 27 km obtained.

ISRO Satellite Centre, Bangalore

Stellar pointing of X-ray Astronomy Experiment on IRS-P3 has been conducted during November 1997 and from May 22 to August 21,1998. Several objects, including blackhole binaries and some newly discovered transient sources, have been observed. Search for new time variabilities in the light curve of these objects is being attempted. Another transient source XTE 1550-56 which had a very high peak flux of 6 crab units during September 1998, has been observed. Data on Vela X-1, a neutron star binary which was observed by IRS-P3, have been analysed. The binary correction to account for the neutron star's movement in the binary orbit around the centre of mass has been completed. The corrected light curve has been computed. A pulse period of 283.24 sec was observed for this object. The pulse profile has been generated as a function of energy in two energy bands. The average pulse profile of this star is being analysed.

Based on the observations of GRS 1915+105, in 1997, further analysis of the bursts observed from this object have been carried out. All regular bursts have two peak structure while the quasi regular and irregular bursts show multi peak structure. The bursts have slow exponential rise and sharp linear decay. In the case of quasi regular and irregular burst, the burst duration is co-related to the quiescent time preceeding the burst.

The Gamma Ray Burst Experiment on board SROSS-C2 has recorded 1073 triggers. Five triggers have been shortlisted as GRB candidate events. The event recorded on March 29, 1998 has been confirmed by the Ulysses GRB detector also. Two separate events were recorded on June 12, 1998 and July 6,1998. Two more events were recorded on June 18, 1998. However, none of these four events has been confirmed by any other satellite.

Optical observations of cataclysmic variables (CVs) have continued at Vainu Bappu Observatory (VBO), Kavalur and Uttar Pradesh State Observatory (UPSO), Nainital. At Kavalur data relating to two intermediate polars; (IPs), namely, RXJ0558+53 and 1H0857-24 were obtained during October-March 1998. During April 1998, ,observations of an interacting binary white dwarf EC 1533-14, as part of the mini Whole Earth Telescope (WET) programme has been carried out from UPSO. A week long observation to survey Rapidly Oscillating A-Peculiar Stars (ROAPS) using UPSO telescope and ISAC instruments in November 1997 has resulted in the discovery of pulsation in the double star HD 13079. A mini 3 star photometer has been built for use at VBO, and UPSO. Development of an all sky monitor using a coded mask has been undertaken. A Solar Spectrometer experiment for studying solar flares in the wide X-ray energy band of 3 keV to 150 keV employing Si (PIN) detector, cadmium zinc telluride detector (low energy detectors) and phoswich detectors (high energy detectors) is being planned.

ISRO geosphere-biosphere programme

ISRO's Geosphere Biosphere Programme was initiated in 1991-92. Over 40 research projects are now in progress at Physical Research Laboratory, Space Applications Centre,

National Remote Sensing Agency, Indian Institute of Remote Sensing, and Space Physics Laboratory. In addition, universities and other research institutions have also been involved under the programme. ISRO-GBP is organised discipline-wise as follows: Climate and Modelling, Minor Constituents and Radiation, Land-Air-Ocean Interactions and Past Climate and Utilisation of MOS/WiFS data for Global Change Studies.

Cryogenic Sampler Payload developed as part of ISRO-GBP for measuring vertical profiles of ozone depleting substances and greenhouse gases has been used for collecting data and the first balloon flight data has been analysed. The data has giver new insights on the abundances of substances such as Methyl Bromide and SF6. Another flight conducted in April 1998 and analysis of data has started. The analyses are being used to monitor increasing abundances of stratospheric chlorine which is the main cause of ozone depletion. A network for measuring surface ozone and its precursor gases has been set up as part of ISRO-GBP at Mt. Abu, Gadanki and Thumba. The analysis of observations has provided valuable results on atmospheric chemistry in the tropics. A data bank for ozone producing substances in the Indian region has been established.

A network of Multi-Wavelength Radiometer (MWR) stations has been established at Thumba, Mysore, Pune, Waltair and Minicoy. In addition, MWR stations are being established at jodhpur and Dibrugarh. The aerosol observation from these stations, together with measurements from sea cruises, has yielded new scientific results. An aerosol data set for about 10 years from three different sites in the Indian region have been collected and used to develop an aerosol climatology for the Indian region.

The ISRO-GBP initiative on landscape ecosystem

studies has provided the basic framework for a national project on biodiversity. Several satellite remote sensing based projects relevant to Global Change have also been completed.

Space science promotion and co-operation

In addition to various research programmes being undertaken at PRL, SPL, ISAC, NMRF, etc., a number of individual joint and co-operative space science investigations are sponsored by DOS involving universities and other research institutions. The Advisory Committee for Space Science (ADCOS) receives proposals in the area of environment, climate, geosphere-biosphere interactions, space astronomy, physics of microgravity, life sciences, aeronomy, planetary atmospheres, etc., from various scientific groups, reviews them and recommends for sponsorship. Many of these projects are implemented through inter-agency sponsorship or as joint co-operative projects with DOS funding. There are special committees for reviewing various space science related activities like Scientific Advisory Committee for National MST Radar Facility (SAC-NMRF), Sounding Rocket Experiment Committee (SOURCE) etc. Recommendations of these committees on scientific proposals are considered by ADCOS before approval.

Consequent to the six day training programme on "Scientific Utilisation of SROSS-C2 data" had been organised at Bangalore during August 5-19,1996, eight research groups from Andhra, Banaras Hindu, Calcutta, Dibrugarh, Kerala, Osmania, Roorkee and Saurashtra universities have been provided facilities to process and analyse the data from the Retarding Potential Analyser (RPA) and Gamma-Ray Burst (GRB.) payloads on-board SROSS-C2 satellite. The data reduction for two years of RPA data have been completed by the participating university groups and the consolidation of data is progressing at National Physical Laboratory, New Delhi. ISRO has taken initiative to organise meetings and scientific workshops to generate proposals on scientific satellite experiments to be taken up during the coming years. Proposals under evaluation include dedicated space science satellite missions to carry out front ranking investigations in the areas of high energy astronomy and astrophysics and low-latitude/equatorial aeronomy. A Climatsat Programme is under Definition. A detailed proposal containing payload specifications, special requirement of orbit, etc., is being worked out jointly by Indian and French groups.

The first phase of Indian Solar Terrestrial Energy Programme (I-STEP), as formulated by the five Scientific Working Groups has been taken up for implementation as a multi-agency funded project. The programme is being carried out with the participation and sponsorship of Department of Science and Technology (DST), Department of Space (DOS), Department of Electronics (DOE), Council of Scientific and Industrial Research (CSIR) and University Grants Commission (UGC) with DST as the nodal agency.

Indian scientists are participating in the international Indian Ocean Experiment (INDOEX) project. INDOEX will have the participation of CSIR, Department of Space, Department of Electronics, and Department of Science and Technology with DOS as the nodal agency. The scientific objective of INDOEX aims towards improving the understanding on the impact of cloud-aerosol-radiation interactive processes for monsoon and related circulation patterns. The second phase of the project started in January 1999 involving ship, aircraft, land and balloon based observations to monitor a number of atmospheric parameters particularly over the region influenced by the Inter Tropical Convergence Zone (ITCZ).

A project to study airspace pollutants and environment has been taken up by a University. Initiatives to promote microgravity research programme among the scientific community has been taken up with a national workshop on 'Material Processing in Space and Space Biotechnology' in 1997. Based on the recommendations of this national workshop three areas of Materials processing in space, Fluid physics, and Space biology and biotechnology are proposed to be taken up as a national microgravity research programme. A Space Astronomy Data Bank for study of compact objects has been funded by DOS to set up at a research centre. DOS is also supporting Augmented Accelerator Mass Spectrometer (AAMS) Facility at Institute of Physics (IOP), Bhubaneswar.

Space Science Data Centre (SSDC) is maintaining and operating various data bases including chose of IMAP, Indo-Russian M-100 rocket programme, stellar spectra from the International Ultraviolet Explorer (IUE) spacecraft, etc. In addition, SSDC has been identified as one of the centres for ISRO-GBP and I-STEP data management systems. SSDC Computer facilities have been made available to scientists to access and analyse the data at the centre in addition to data dissemination services. The data centre is also offering off-line data processing facility for MST radar observations. The SROSS-C2 data archival in CD ROM has also been initiated.

National MST Radar Facility (NMRF)

National Mesosphere-Stratosphere-Troposphere (MST) Radar Facility (NMRF) is an autonomous society under Department of Space and the facility is available to scientists from various institutions to conduct advanced research in atmospheric and space sciences. It was set up at Gadanki near Tirupati with funding from the

Department of Electronics, Defence Research and Development Organisation, Department of Environment and the Council of Scientific and Industrial Research besides the Department of Space which was the nodal agency for the establishment of NMRF.

A variety of scientific experiments/campaigns have been carried out during the year using MST radar and Lower Atmospheric Wind Profile (LAWP) systems. The common mode observation programme has completed two years of observations.

MST radar is capable of making high resolution wind measurements. Two diurnal cycles of observations are carried out every month in the evening under common mode observation programme to build a long term database; Two years of data is now available. The long-term database will not only be useful for scientific studies of long period waves but also for supporting satellite launches from SHAR Centre, Sriharikota.

The major scientific studies and measurements conducted during the year are as follows:

Atmospheric waves which are mostly generated in the troposphere are known to transport energy and momentum from troposphere to higher attitudes. As these waves propagate through the tropopause they may induce temporal variation in height and structure of tropopause. MST radar wind observations and simultaneous temperature measurements using Radiosonde at Chennai provided evidence of tropopause oscillations. It is shown that energy associated with atmospheric waves are significantly attenuated as they propagate through tropopause.

MST radar wind measurements have been used to compute momentum flux for Kelvin and Rossby gravity waves. These fluxes in upper troposphere are noticed to be in the range of 5.5 to 16x10-3 m-2s-1 which are higher than the value reported earlier. This result is important for understanding coupling between troposphere and stratosphere.

Observations of occurrence of mesospheric echoes has shown distinct layer structures around the height range of 67-69 km and 73-75 km with a diffused cloud like structure around 85 km. The observed echoes are noted to be intermittent and they do not show any aspect sensitivity. This implies presence of 3 m scale turbulence in low latitude mesosphere.

Recent observations of E-region field-aligned irregularities (FAI) have shown quasiperiodic echoes resulting from the gravity wave modulation of FAI. The gravity spectrum has dominant periods of 20-30 min. A method has been developed to derive meridional neutral wind from the E region FAI observations below height of about 95 km. Fine scale structures with vertical wavelength of 1 to 2 km are observed using high spatial and temporal resolution of 150 m and 25 m.

Using MST radar in the Spatial Domain Interferometry mode (SDI), studies of ionospheric irregularities have been made. Using the coherence and phase plots, the aspect sensitivity of the individual irregularity and total angular extent of the backscatter from the field aligned irregularity (FAI) have been derived. Time variation of the phase has, in turn, been utilised to obtain horizontal drift velocity in the meridional plane. SDI technique has also been applied to the studies of turbulence generated by meteors.

Algorithms have been developed based on higher order spectral analysis. One of the important application of the technique is detection and estimation of signal generated through nongaussion processes with additive gaussion noise of unknown covariance.

In addition to LAWP system, a Disdrometer and a highly sensitive Optical Rain Gauge (ORG) have been installed in . collaboration with Communication Research Laboratory, Japan. Addition of these facilities has strengthened lower atmosphere observations and meteorology related studies. Another major facility that has been installed at NMRF under Indo-Japanese collaboration is a Rayleigh/ Mie Lidar. This facility also complements MST radar by providing information on Aerosols in the troposphere/lower stratosphere and air density and temperature in the MST Radar gap region of 30-60 km.

Development of a new digital signal processing system for the MST radar is planned to enable coverage of larger height range and uninterrupted data acquisition. It is also proposed to add Radio Acoustic Sounding System (RASS) facility to Lower Atmospheric Wind Profiler (LAWP) system for making high resolution temperature measurements along with the wind, turbulence and precipitation measurements.

Future prospects

With the number of telephones in India aggregating to a mere 5.8 million to service a population of over 850 million people, telecommunications is an industry of tremendous growth potential. It is also one of the most profitable business areas in India today with the pay back on a line being only two years.

The new Ministry of Communication has drawn up a very ambitious 26 point program for this Industry. Some of the highlights are that private participation has been invited for building and operation of telecom networks in 'growth centres and satellite towns'.

In the new Industrial Policy, telecom equipment was delicenced and thrown open to foreign investment. Several joint ventures came up- GPI and K.K. Birla,

Ericcson with their long term collaborators the Jiwarajkars, AT&T with Tata Telecom, Fujitsu with the Punjab State Electronic Production and Development Corporation and Alcatel with B.K. Modi. Of these companies gearing up to meet the indigenous requirements, the last two are near ready to commence production of equipment to meet the specifications set out by the Department of Telecommunications.

The Ministry of Communication has in October this year allowed eight private companies to establish cellular telephone systems in the four metropolitan cities kof Delhi, Bombay, Calcutta and Madras. In each of the four metros, the two private companies would operate the system along with their two foreign partners. Tenders are expected to be floated soon inviting private manufacturers to set up value-added celluler telephone systems in other secondary cities in the country. Mobile telephones will be made available against foreign exchange payment. Video conferencing, Email, Radio Paging and other value added services and manufacturing of ten thousand line exchanges, will be available to joint/private sector without licensing (capacity) regulation.

Until now only terminal equipment and PABX manufacturing was permitted in private sector subject to lecensing.

New Import Export Policy

A new Import-Export Policy was announced on 1st April, 1992. The policy statement eliminated a number of import categories, exceptions and exemptions, special lists, open lists etc. The new 5 year exim policy makes trade "free" subject to a small negative list. Even the short negative list which prohibits import of certain items is likely to be curtailed further during the year.

The Finance Minister, Dr. Manmohan Singh, while inaugurating the International Asia Pacific Conference on private sector has stated that "bureaucratic controls would be fully dismantled, quantitative import restrictions phased out and customs tariff reduced to international levels to make the private sector vibrant."

Collaboration by non-Small Scale Industrial units for items reserved for the SSI sector is allowed subject to the condition that the firms concerned would undertake to export at least 75% of its output. Applications for 100% EOUs are cleared by the SIA and those for 100% Export Processing Zone (EPZ) units are cleared by the Development Commissioner of the particular EPZ, subject to the guidelines aplicable to such units.

Export obligations are no longer imposed in other cases of collaboration. Instead, the export offers made by the applicants are taken note of as being in the nature of a gentlemen's agreement, and are not linked to legal or bank guarantees. Their fulfilment is a matter of trust, and not compulsion.

The Government has liberalised the guidelines for * automatic approval in 30 days for all cases involving an equity of upto US $ two million.

The Government has initiated steps to deregulate the domestic civil aviation industry and bring an end to the public sector monopoly in domestic civil aviation. The Ministry of Civil Aviation has proposed to withdraw the three major constraints on private taxi operators namely:

- Restriction on level of fare.
- Route restriction.
- Flight time restriction.

The ministry has given support to the 'open sky policy' for air taxi licenses in India. Selling Indian airlines or Air India is however not on the immediate agenda.

Liberalisation and 'open sky policy' has opened the vast domestic market to new scheduled airlines in India. There are 22 registered private airlines of which a few are already operational. The most notable being East West Airlines which has already acquired 3% of the total domestic market, that was till now monopolised by Indian Airlines.

The ministry of Civil Aviation and Tourism has recently invited foreign capital and technology for 'collaborative partnership' for an "integrated development of the Indian aviation industry".

'Liberalisation window to opportunities was the theme of the 41st annual convention of the Travel Agents' Association of Inida, held at Hydrabad recently.

Many interesting facts emerged during the convention. Partial convertibility has made visiting India and even shopping an inexpensive proposition. For example, there is a charactered flight every day from Uzbekistan carrying 240 passengers stopping at New Delhi for a day of shopping!

In a radical departure form the Industrial Policy of 1956, the Union Government has announced that it will allow 100% foreign equity participation for setting up of power plants in India. It has also permitted substantial modification in the Electricity (Supply) Act 1948 to hasten the private sector's participation in the ailing power sector.

These two decisions have been taken by the cabinet and the bill containing the amendments in the Electricity (Supply) Act and the 100% foreign equity participation proposals will be tabled soon before the Parliament.

The 100% foreign equity participation proposals allows free repatriation of profits and other incentives. Besides, it will facilitate foreign parties to set up power plants without time delays, which are solely responsible for the cost escalation in the power projects.

Proposals from foreign investors for new power units are expected to be cleared through a high powered committee. The domestic private company's proposals will be cleared through a single window to minimise bureaucratic and other delays. The Government is likely to invite various foreign consortia including non-resident Indians (NRI's), particularly those in Japan and the UK to come forward.

Since the 1960's, the two public sector companies, Oil & Natural Gas Commission (ONGC) and Oil India Limited have held a monopoly over oil exploration in India. ONGC is seeking a change of its status to an autonomous corporation with the freedom to raise its resources directly from markets in India and overseas. It is prepared to enter into new projects such as country wide gas grid in collaboration with the private sector. It is understood that 73 drilling and exploratory blocks have been offered to international oil companies through international tendering. The Government has invited offers for joint ventures to develop designated medium-sized as also small sized oil and gas fields offering a range of incentives. Companies may singly or as a consortium bid by the 31st December 1992. Major tax concessions are made both for Indian and foreign companies engaged in oil exploitation. Income Tax will be levied at a flat rate of 50% without surcharge as against 65% now applicable to foreign companies in other businesses.

The Government has accorded status of importance to the Bombay High oil producing belt in the Arabian Sea and initiated highly sophisticated defence procedures for safeguarding the rigs from aggression.

Potential estimates claim that India should produce 70 metric tonnes of crude per annum by 1999 and will be considered a major economic power of the next century.

The rate of tax applicable to foreign companies continue to be 65%. Surcharge is not levied in the case of non-resident assessees.

Section 80 HHC of Income Tax Act 1961 provides for 100% exemption from income tax if the entire business income is generated from exports. The deductions available to an assessee involved in exports in now to be calculated on a new formula. The formula makes a distinction between a manufacturer exporter and a trading exporter. The actual deduction is calculated taking into consideration the FOB value of the exports as against the turnover and profits/gains of the business.

Under the provisions of Section 80-0, 50% of technical services fees, royalties etc derived under an approved agreement are deductible from income. This concession which was available to Indian corporate bodies has now been extended to non corporate bodies. This concession has been granted with the prupose of encouraging professionals such as architects, accountants etc to earn foreign exchange for the country. Further clarifications are expected from the Government on how this scheme would be applied to professionals as prior approval of agreements may be very difficult to administer.

Some immediate effects of the changes outlined above can be seen from the following events:

— As early as April 1992, a 1243% increase in foreign investment has been registered in India since the announcement of the liberalised industrial policy in July 1991.

— Foreign Collaborations in India recently approved by the Indian Government include companies like General Motors, General Electric, Coca Cola, Suzuki, Leasaffre (French), GERB (German), Buhler (Swiss), IBM, BMW, Ford etc. In the communication sector, AT&T, Siemens, France and British Telecom have shown keen interest in bidding for setting up cellular phone networks in India.

— 100 senior Japanese business executives spent a week in India in February 1992 and Nomura Securities Company has established a presence in Delhi. The opening of a trading office of a securities house in known to be a major jumping off point for further investment in India.

— 200 foreign participants attended the Euromoney conference in Delhi on "Business, Finance and Investment in India" in the last week of March, 1992.

New Horizons

In the recent few months, with the Bombay Stock Market Scandal in which banks and financial institutions stand to lose upto Rs. 30 billion, inflation running upto 13% on occasions and other regional and national political problems, the feeling has been that the Government is now in the danger of letting opportunities slip away. The Government did announce de-licensing of the electronic industry, liberalisation which would permit foreign financial institutions to invest in India and permission to open branch offices by foreign companies in the last few months to counter the allegations that there has been a slow down in the economic reform process. Although there may be some truth in this allegation the process of liberalisation has certainly not stopped. The Government has given an assurance that it will endeavour to proceed with the intended further liberalisation as promised.

On the whole, along with devaluation of the rupee in June 1991, the new trade policy and the further reforms promised includding full convertibility of the rupee, if the new Industrial Policy and its effect does turn out to what it promises to be, new horizons will open. This should lead to faster growth of industries in India. Indian industries would be open and accessible to the world. The opening up of new areas such as air transportation and power generation for private sector participation will result in opportunities for contractors and financial institutions to bid for project and asset work. The feeling in India is that a clear signal has been sent to industrialists, both local and foreing, that the government really means business. The radical nature of the industrial policy has met and continues to meet some resistance from the bureaucratic machinery which it seeks to dismantle. Its fine print still requires further clarifications. But more important than the fine print is the inescapable fact the political power has finally recognised that it is time for a new order to emerge. For some, their efforts may have fallen short of expectations, but the Government has acted, at last.

This update has been prepared by Thakker & Thakker Solicitors & Advocates, Bombay, for the AIJA 1992 conference in Bombay on "Emerging Investment Opportunities in India". The Update is necessarily of general nature and seeks to provide information only on some of the major changes announced by the Government and cannot be regarded as legal advice.

Status of the Indian Telecom Network

India today operates one of the largest telecom networks in Asia comprising

— Over 20 172 telephone exchanges;
— About 118 400 route kms of coaxial terrestrial UHF/

microwave radio relay systems up to 140 Mbit/s apart from analogue systems;

— 23 300 kilometres of optical fibre systems comprising of systems up to 565Mb/s;

— 50 per cent of Transmission network is digitalised.

About 7 700 cities and towns are connected to the National Subscriber Dialling (NSD) network and the Department of Telecommunications (DOT) plans to extend the facility to all automatic exchanges by 1997.

Fully automatic International Subscriber Diallilng (ISD) service is available to 237 countries through two international earth stations and submarine cable systems. Trunk manual service is also available to all countries.

To meet the low speed data communication needs of Business/industrial units in Remote and far flung areas, a Business. Message Network (RABMN) with a hub-station near Delhi, having a capacity of 1000 subscribers has been commissioned. About 456 Very Small Aperture Terminals (VSAT) are deployed in this network for providing data service at maximum speeds up to 9.6kbits.

A dedicated Packet Switched Public Data Network (PSPDN), with international access for computer communication services is available in the country with speeds up to 2Mbit/s.

For providing international connectivity, a Gateway Packet Switching System (GPSS), is available which offers the capability of sophisticated telecommunication networking terminals and computers internationally.

INSAT satellite systems are being used to provide over 4126 two-way speech circuits through 165 earth stations across the length and breadth of the country. In 1975, the government of India took a decision to have its system for meeting domestic communication needs of the country and approved the scheme in 1977 for the multi purpose Indian National Satellite System (INSAT).

The INSAT-I series of satellites, comprising four satellites were launched in 1982, 1983, 1988 and 1990 respectively. INSAT-II series of the satellites comprising four satellites in orbit and one ground spare, are being manufactured indigenously. Under this series, INSAT-IIA was launched in July 1992 and INSAT-IIB Satellite was launched in July 1993.

The present space segment comprises of * INSAT IIA and IIB Satellites in orbit. The ground segment of INSAT-ID & INSAT-IIA, IIB comprises of 82 fixed Satellite earth stations. In addition to the above, 29 satellite earth stations have been commissioned as captive networks to meet the telecommunication needs of Government undertakings.

Besides above fixed satellite earth stations the ground segment also comprises 23 mobile terminals including three Flyaway Terminals. These terminals are capable of being transported to different parts of the country by road/air to restore the telecommunication services as well as to meet an urgent telecommunication need from any part of the country. There are also nine special routes/networks.

About 185000 villages out of 604 734 villages are provided with telecommunications facililties;

There were 2.5 telephones per 1000 population in the rural areas at the end of march 1995, as against the figure of 107 in the country as a whole. These figures are expected to become 3.00 and 15.00 respectively by the year 1997 as per the modest government investment. Private sector participation, which is expected shortly, will raise telephone density considerably.

The total equipped capacity of the Indian local network is 12 million with over 10 million main lines. There has been a rise of 25 per cent in telephone traffic in 1991-1992 and 35 per cent in 1992-1993 as compared to the previous year.

The pending demand however is 215 million and is growing at over 20 per cent per annum. In the past the registered demand has grown at a rate of 10 to 13 per cent per annum while the supply remained between 9 to 10.5 per cent. As a consequence the waiting list has grown. Over the last two years, we have stepped up the growth rate to 15 per cent per annum to see a slight dip in the demand.

The Indian Telecommuinications network provides nearly 400 000 Long Distance Switching Circuits with 94 per cent digitization.

A number of state-of-the-art switching technologies have been inducted in Indian network, ie FETEX 150, EWSD, AXE 10, No.5 ESS, OCB 283, System X, NEAX 61E and the indigenous CDoT.

Enhancement of capacity and digitalization of the transmission network is being carried out with optical fibre, digital microwaves and satellite.

A great emphasis is being laid on R&D of sophisticated digital switching and transmission equipment to meet india's urban and rural needs. The Centre for Development of Telematics (C-DoT) has successfully designed a family of digital-SPC switching systems from small to large main automatic exchanges.

Technology for several transmission products such as 10 channel UHF-600 MHz, 2/8 and 8/34 Digital mux, Satellite Based Rural Telegraph Network (SBRTN) Single Channel VHF and 2/8 Mbit/s OLTE has also been indigenously developed by CDoT and technology successfully transferred to a large number of local manufacturers. CDoT technology has also been offered to other countries as well.

Value added services are being indigenously developed exchanges through introduction of better signalling features such as Common Channel Signalling No. 7 and through ISDN.

The ultimate goal of R&D units is however to lead to the development of an Intergrated Services Digital Network (ISDN) and eventually to Broadband ISDN (B-ISDN) through Synchronous Digital Hierachy (SDH). Digital Access Cross Connect System (DACCS), Asynchronous Transport Module (ATM) etc.

There is a Telecommunications Engineering Centre (TEC) for issuing of specifications, type approvals, interface approvals and evaluation of new telecom products and for standardisation.

Over the years, the Department of Telecom, have built up extensive training facilities starting at the apex with Advanced Level Telecommunications Training Centre, near Delhi, set up with the systems and support of the UNDP and ITU.

The Telecommunications Training Centre at Jabalpur and 11 Regional and 25 State and District Level Training Centres also provides extensive training facilities. India has been extending assistance to Asia and Pacific countries too in meeting their training needs in the high tech areas of telecommunications.

Through DOT's consultancy group known as Telecommunication Consultancy India Limited (TCIL), India has been offering a wide spectrum of consultancy services in the international arena.

These include technical and management support, training, inspection, rehabilitation, modernization of existing systems, techno-economic studies in the core sectors of engineering and design studies, besides construction management and electronic data processing etc.

The consultancy services, include feasibility studies, network design studies, software support, installation, testing and commissioning of switching systems and transmission systems, operation and maintenance of networks.

TCIL has executed various contracts abroad and has been operating in about 28 countries.

The Indian Telegraph (Amendment) Bill, 1995

The National Telecom Policy 1994, has inter-alia laid emphasis on achieving the universal service, bringing the quality of Telecom service to world standard, provision of the widest permissible range of services to meet the customer's demand at reasonable price and participation of the companies registered in India in the area of basic telecom services as also making arrangements for protection and promotion of consumers' interest and ensuring fair competition. The Department of Telecomomunications feel that to achieve these objectives, there is need to separate regulatory functions from service providing functions which will be in keeping with the prevailing general trend in the world. It has, therefore, proposed to set up an independent Telecom Regulatory Authority to be called 'Telecom Regulatory Authority of India' which, to begin with, will be non-statutory in character but will have well defined functions and responsibilities and powers to play the role of a watch-dog body for the Telecom sector in an effective manner.

The Indian Telegraph Act, 1885 regulates the functioning of Telecommunications services in the country. Under Section 4 of the Indian Telegraph Act, 1885, the Central Government has the exclusive right of establishing, maintaining and working telegraphs and under the first provision of this section, it may grant a licence on such conditions and in consideration of such payment as it thinks fit to any persons to establish, maintain or work a telegraph within any part of the country. Under Section 4(2) of the Act, the Central Government may by notification in the Official Gazette delegate to the Telegraph Authority all or any of its powers under the first proviso to subsection (1). Section 3(6) of the Indian Telegraph Act, 1885 describes Director General (Posts and Telegraphs) as the Telegraph Authority and includes any officer empowered by him to perform all or any of the functions of the Telegraph Authority under the Act. Presently, the Secretary, Department of Telecommunications who has been notified as the Director General Telecommunications in his capacity as a Telegraph Authority exercises regulatory powers and performs regulatory functions as delegated by the Central Government under the Indian Telegraph Act, 1885. In order to vest the powers of the Telegraph Authority with the proposed Regulatory Authority in respect of certain assigned functional areas. It has become necessary to amend Section 3(6) of the Indian Telegraph Act, 1885 by including "any statutory or non-statutory authority".

The secretary, Department of Telecommunications stated in evidence that at present all the regulatory authority under the Indian Telegraph Act is exercised by the Secretary, Department of Telecommunications. This power of the telegraph authority can be further delegated by him to another officer of the Government. It cannot be delegated t , a statutory or a non-statutory authority as such. So, the basic purpose of the proposed amendment of Section3(6) of the Indian Telegraph Act, 1885 is to delegate certain regulatory powers of the Telegraph authority to the proposed Telecom Regulatory Authority.

The Secretary, Department of Telecommunications further clarified that the reasons for not coming up with a comprehensive Bill to setup a statutory with independent powers at this stage, are that the Government would like to watch the working of such an authority for a year or two and learn from such an experience. After getting the feed-back from the Chairman and Members of the authority and various interest groups viz, operators and subscribers etc., it would frame a comprehensive law to make it a statutory authority. Then the authority will derive its powers directly from an Act of Parliament.

The witness further told the Committee that "the need for amendment is based not only on Government perceptions of the local market but also arises from the international experience that wherever there has been a situation of more than one player in the market scene, a need has been felt for an independent umpire. The current trend in the telecommunication sector the world-over is to distance policy making functions, operational functions and regulatory functions from each other and to entrust regulatory functions to an independent Regulatory Authority for regulating Telecom services".

The Secretary, Department of Telecommunications informed the Committee that in due course the proposed authority would be independent and autonomous; it would operate outside the Government, at arm's length from the Government so that it could inspire the confidence of various operators as well as the subscribers. He further added that for this purposes the intention of the Government is to ensure that it is manned by people of eminence and independent views. Therefore, the Cabinet has decided that it would be chaired by a retired or a serving Chief Justice of a High Court or a retired or a serving Judge of the Supreme Court and it will have two members who should have worked in the State Government or the Central Government in a position not lower than the position of an additional Secretary to Government of India for a period of three years. These Members would enjoy the status of Secretary to Govt. of India. It was further stated that the tenure of the Chairman and the Members would be secure and protected. Their removal will require the same safeguards as are available to Judges of the Supreme Court. Similarly their emoluments and other terms and conditions of service would not be changed to their disadvantage. The Secretary Department of Telecommunications stated that the apparent idea was to send across a strong signal that there would be an authority who would act independently, impartially, in an objective manner to protect the interests of the operators as also of the subscribers.

Clarifying the position further in reply to a query by the Committee, the Secretary, Deptt. of Telecommunications stated that soon after the amendment of law, two things would follow. Firsts that Department of Telecommunications would set up this authority by means of a Resolution of the Government. Secondly the Department would issue a notification that the authority set up under that Resolution is vested with the powers of the Director-General of Telecommunications under Section 4 of the Indian Telegraph Act in respect of certain matters. Once that is done, the authority would be clothed with the powers of Telegraph Authority in relation to its are a of work.

However, it would still be a creature of the executive arm of the Government. Later after an year or so it will come before the Parliament with a comprehensive Bill.

In reply to a query regarding the impact of Telecom Regulatory Authority after its inception on working of Telecom Network in the country, the Ministry informed that it was excepted that the Telecom Regulatory Authority would have healthy impact on the working of telecom services in the country, since it will act as a watch dog for telecom sector, ensure level playing field as also monitor quality of services and protect and promote the consumer interest.

Asked whether after setting up the Authority, it would be possible for Government to set aside any decision of the proposed Authority, the Secretary Deptt. of telecoommunications replied in negative. He further added that the intention was that there would be not right of appeal to the executive wing of the Government. The orders issued by the proposed Telecom Regulatory Authority can only be challenged before the High Court or the Supreme Court.

In the light of the Government view known to the Committee, the Committee agree with the amendment of Section 3(6) of Indian Telegraph Act, 1885 for inclusion of any statutory or non-statutory authority within the definition of Telegraph Authority and support the Bill. The Committee hope that steps will be taken to set up a statutory Authority.

Science & Technology Development

The investment in Research and Development. (R & D) has increased from a paltry Rs. 20 crore in the First Five Year Plan. Presently there are 214 universities, 400 national laboratories and 1300 in-house R & D centres in the industrial sector. Several Science & Technology departments have been set up in the areas of environment, non-conventional energy resources, bio-technology, ocean development, industrial research, space, atomic energy, defence, health, agriculture and electronics.

Identification and promotion of priority areas in R & D is done by Science an Engineering Research Council (SERC) set up under the Department of Science & Technology (DST). DST supports 12 autonomous research insitutions as well, for furthering research work in several discipline. Technology Information, Forecasting and Assessment Council (TIFAC) has been set up for generating technology forecasting and technology assessment documents and enabling a technology information system that is interactive and nationally accessible.

Industrial research in several diverse fields of scientific activity is being undertaken through a network of 40 laboratories and 81 field stations set up by the Council for Scientific and Industrial Research (CSIR). In the field of bio-technology, more than 24 specialised R & D centres have been developed for pursuing state-of-the-art research. Identical efforts for promoting new avenues of research are being undertaken in the field of ocean development as well.

The Union Budget for 1996-97 has taken various measures to promote R & D facilities. A matching one time grant has been awarded to CSIR and the Indian Council of Agricultural Research (ICAR) for modernisation of laboratories and institutes. The Technology Development and Application Fund created in 1995-96 has been proposed to be strengthened by Rs. 30 crore. A Five Year Tax Holiday under Section 80-IA of the Income Tax Act has been allowed to companies exclusively create for participation in R & D activities.

The existing procedure for awarding weighted deduction under Section 35(2AA) of the Income Tax Act on sums paid for scientific research to a National Laboratory or a University or an IIT has been amended, by deleting the condition of approval by an outside body. In order to encourage R & D efforts, goods developed and patented in India and concurrently in specified countries have been exempted from levy of excise duty for a period of 3 years. The exemption procedure for customs duty on import of equipment and consumables for R & D institutions has been rationalised as well.

Private Sector Partcipation

The Value added service sector has been open to the private sector since 1992. In respect of value added services, except radio paging and mobile telephony services, companies registered in India are permitted to operate under licence on non exclusive basis. In the area of Radio paging and Cellular Mobile Telephone Services, however, a policy of selection is being followed in the granting of licences through a system of tendering.

A tender for operation of radio paging services in 27 cities was earlier invited and 14 companies have been granted operating licences. For other areas of the country comprising 19 territorial telecom circles, tenders have been invited, and licensing is being progressively done. Commercial service has been started in 22 cities by one or more operators to over 48,000 subscribers and in the rest of the five cities the service will start very soon.

Eight companies have been selected for the franchises of cellular mobile service in the four metro cities namely Bombay, Delhi, Calcutta and Madras. In respect of rest of the country, a tender had been invited. The evaluation of 33 bids for the 20 telecommunications circles, is expected to be completed shortly. Service has commenced in Calcutta and Delhi in September 1995.

With a view to supplement the efforts of Department of Telecommunications in providing telecommunication services to the people, 81 bids received for grant of licence for operation of basic services in 20 telecom Circles are now under evaluation.

The government has decided to create an autonomous Telecom Regulatory body called the Telecom Regulatory Authority of India (TRAI). This will have well defined functions, responsibilities and powers to play the role of a watch-dog body for the telecommunications sector in an effective manner. The Authority will regulate its procedure for conduct of business with the approval of the government and will be expected to ensure transparency and accountability.

Profound changes are taking place in Telecommunication sector the world over and India is no exception. The Government of India has taken bold initiatives to liberalise and expand the telecom network in the country.

Some of the milestones in this direction are:

— 1984

Manufacture of Customer Premises Equipment delicensed.

— 1991

New Industrial Policy permitting private sector to manufacture all types of telecommunications equipment.

Other salient features are:

No industrial Licence is required;

Automatic approval of foreign equity investment up to 51 per cent in the case of manufacturing projects:

Automatic approval of foreign collaboration in the case of telecommunications sector with technology fees up to Rs. 10 million net of taxes and/or royalty up to five per cent for domestic sales and/or eight per cent for exports.

The possibility for more than 51 per cent foreign equity and higher technology fees/royalty in manufacturing projects through special approvals;

All foreign investment proposals for telecommunications services require the specific approval to the Government of India.

1992

Value added services thrown open to private sector participation.

1994

New National Telecommunications Policy allowing private sector participation in basic services announced.

The National Telecommunications Policy announced by the Government would be instrumental in bringing about phenomenal expansion and improvement in the telecom sector.

The objectives of the Telecommunications Policy are:

— providing Telecommunications for all and Telecommunications within the reach of all;

— Universal Service Obligation at affordable and reasonable price;

— Providing telecommunications services of world standard;

— To ensure that India emerges as a major manufacturing base and major exporter of telecom equipment.

The targets laid down in the policy are as follows:

— Telephones to be available on demand by 1997;
— All vjillages to be provided with telecommunications services by 1997;
— In urban areas a Public Calling Office (PCO) should be provided for every 500 persons by 1997;
— Special emphasis on the quality of telecoommunications services provided to the customers will be given;
— All value added services available internationally to be introduced in India, preferably by 1996.

The other important aspects of the policy are:

— Private initiative would be used to supplement the departmental efforts to raise additional resources both through increased internal generation and adopting innovative means, like, leasing, deferred payments, build-operate-and-transfer, build-lease-and-transfer.
— A suitable funding mechanism for indigenous R&D is proposed to be set up;
— Pilot projects will be encouraged directly by the government in order to access new technologies, new systems in both basic as well as value added services.

With low telephone penetration rates, India represents one of the world's most attractive markets for telecommunications service providers and equipment manufacturers. Service sector opening of the basic telecom services to the private sector is the biggest opportunity for foreign direct investment. The growth potential in the basic telephone service in India is tremendous taking into consideration the low telephone density at present.

The challenge in rural telecommunications in India is indeed quite formidable. Out of the 604 734 villages in the country, only 185000 have telephone facility. Over 420,000 villages are still without a telephone facility.

Under the National Telecommunications Policy, one public telephone will be provided in each of the over half a million villages by 1997. Provisioning of a single telephone in each village, as per the telecom policy, may involve an investment of the order of S billion US Dollars. The sub-sector of value added services is already open for private investment. This sector in India represents one of the world's largest opportunities for supply of services and equipment.

The Indian Switching market, which is estimated to increase from about 2.5 million lines now to over 3.00 million lines in 1996-1997 represents-one of the largest market in the Asian region. The digital switching markets in India has witnessed a true metamorphosis since 1991 when the new Industrial Policy was announced by the Government.

A number of foreign companies attracted by DOT's liberalised procurement policies, have set up local production ventures in India. The opening up of the Import Policy in 1992 has opened this largest market to international competition.

The market for providing private networks is also growing very fast. Major international companies have already announced their plans for making an entry in this market.

The Radio Transmission Equipment market in India has undergone extensive changes in the post industrial liberallization period. With the diversification or production of transmission equipment which was earlier limited to the public sector companies, the present production base has expand with the setting up of the manufacturing facilities in the private sector.

With the opening up of Microwave Radio systems to competition, a number of multinational companies have entered the radio equipment market. The digital microwave radio equipment market has potential for large investments since most of the radio frequency spectrum in microwave is still available for deployment.

The investment opportunities in the optical fibre cable and equipment as well as infrastrucure equipment for value added services such as cellular and paging are immense. With the possibility of the entire long distance network being converted to optical fibre media, a number of international companies are getting their products validated at present. The investment opportunities in this area are extremely good.

Another area expected to sustain great demand in the coming decade is VSATs with voice transmission. The steady increase in the number of customers demanding high bit rate data transmission and separate corporate networks has given spur to VSAT development.

With increased availability, VSAT services are likely to get a big push and, therefore, the opportunities in this sector are excellent.

— The gross receipts of the Department of Post during the year 1995-96 were Rs. 1150 crore. Gross working expenses were Rs. 2472 crore and net working expenses Rs. 1810 crore. there was, therefore, a deficit of Rs. 660 crore. During the year 1996-97, as per budget estimates, the gross receipts are expected at Rs. 1350 crore and gross working expenses at Rs. 2616 crore. With net working expenses at Rs. 1962 crore the deficit is estimated at Rs. 612 crore for 1996-97. (BE).

— The Budget of Department of Post has been in deficit continuously over the years, and no dividend is being paid to the general revenue. Modernisation activities, through inductin of new technoloy, has been initiated on a modest scale during the current plan. Its further expansion and spread during the next plan, are likely to improve the service efficiency. A modernised postal system should also be able to provide new value added services to yield revenue. Low tariff on most of the postal services for many years, and inadiquate agency charges for agency functions, are the main factors for the deficit. However, a moderate increase in some of the services i.e., printed postcard from 60 paise to 100 paise and registration fee from Rs. 6.00 to Rs. 8.00 and introduction of cmpetition postcard at Rs. 2.00 each is expected to yield additional revenue to the tune of Rs. 76 crore in a full financial year. The degree of subsidy, as indicated in Table 2.11 ranges from about 1 per cent in respected of money orders to 92 per cent on postcard.

— The network owned and operated by the Department of Telecommunications (DOT) has been generating surpluses, which is utilised for further exapansion of the net work. Net receipts increased to Rs. 4951 crore in 1995-96 (RE) from Rs. 3936 crore in 1994-95 reflecting an increase of 25.8 per cent. Net receipts are estimated at Rs. 5213 crore in 1996-97 (BE). The dividend contribution to the general revenues increased to Rs. 279 crore in 1995-96 (RE) from Rs. 270 crore in 1994-95. The operating ratio, which is a percentage of net operating expenses (excluding the provision for redemption of bonds) to operating revenue earned (excluding registration fee) has come down to 48.7 in 1995-96 (RE) from 48.8 in 1994-95. The plan outlay for Telecommunication

Services (including all PSUs) for the year 1996-97 (BE) is marginally higher at Rs. 9874 crore from Rs. 9830 crore in 1995-96 (RE). The entire outlay (except Rs. 5.00 crore pertaining to WMo etc. which is by way of budgetary support) is to be financed from the internal accruals and extra budgetary resources of the Telecommunication sector. Internal accruals amounting to Rs. 7491 crore account for 75.9 per cent of total resources against 79.6 per cent in 1995-96 (RE).

— Though the telecom network in India is fairly large in absolute terms, (in 1994 it was ranked fourteenth in the world) yet the tele density was 1.4 per cent in March, 1996. An advanced and efficient telecommunications system can enhance international competitiveness of the economy. The DOT has been increasing the quantum of resources deployed for the development of the telecom infrastructure, although the pattern of financing has undergoes a sea change. During the first plan DOT received budgetary support which accounted for around 79 per cent of the total resouces deployed it. In the Eighth Plan, 78.7 per cent is expected from internal accruals, 21 per cent from borrowings and other sources, and only 0.3 per cent from budgetary support. In the coming years, substantial investment would be required to upgrade and expand the existing telecom network. The aggregate resource requirements for the provision of basic and cellular mobile telecom services as estimated bny the Expert Group on Commercialisation of Infrastruture Projects is placed at Rs. 1,91,500 crore by 2006. Thee estimates are at todays prices and duty structure.

— Of late, DOT has primarily relied on internal accruals. However, to meet its targets of network expansion, DOT will have to look to a larger resource pool. It will have to devise a tariff structure which largely reflects the cost oriented approach, subject to country's social obligations and thrusts.

— A corporate structure for the DOT will enable it to leverage its substantial assets and raise adequate funds to meet all its investment needs. Corporate structure would make DOT into an autonomous entity owned by the Government. In the short and medium term, the government will remain the dominant operator and provider of telecom services in the countrty. However, with the advent of private operators, the present tariff regime should orient as quickly as possible towards a costbased structure. It is imperative to have the tariffs reviewed to allocate costs for various services and identify the need, if any, of subsidies.

— As per the revised estimates for 1995-96, the total expenditure on Broadcasting was Rs. 974 crore as against total receipts of Rs. 549 crore. This shows an increase of 19 per cent and 20.4 per cent in total expenditure and receipts, respectively. As a result, the ratio of total receipts to total expenditure improved from 55.8 per cent in 1994-95 to 56.4 per cent in 1995-96. The rising trend in commercial receipts in broadcasting activity over the past few years is indicative of efforts being made in this direction. Commercial receipts were Rs. 426 crore in 1993-94, Rs. 450 crore in 1994-95, and Rs. 540 crore in 1995-96 (RE). Further break up of commercial receipts brings to the fore the overwhelming contribution of Doordarshan towards revenue generation. The commercial receipts in case of Doordarshan were Rs. 363 crore in 1993-94, Rs. 384 crore in 1994-95 and Rs. 460 crore in 1995-96.

— The important place commanded by India in world trade in coffee, tea, leather and spices on a historical basis has continued in recent years as wll. In 1994, India accounted for 2.4 per cent, 13.6 per cent, 2.5 per cent and 9.1 per cent of world trade in coffee and coffee substitues, tea and mate, leather, and spices, respectively. Furthermore, there has been a significant progress in export diversification, and India has emerged as an important exporter of iron ore and concentrates, and pearis, precious and semi-precious stones. In 1994, India accounted for 6 per cent or world exports of iron ore and concentrates and 10.9 per cent of world exports of pearls, precious and semi precious stones (Source: 1994 United Nations International Trade Statistics Year Book, 1995).

— During 1950, India accounted for about 1.8 per cent (1.85 per cent of exports and 1.71 per cent of imports) of world trade. After gradually declining to 0.57 per cent by 1980, India's share improved marginally to 0.63 per cent by 1985. The reason for improvement in the share was that while world trade declined in the period 1980-85, India's trade continued to grow. However it came down again to 0.53 per cent by 1991. The first half of the nineties witnessed a sharp increase in India's exports and imports have grown in dollar terms annually by 12.4 per cent and 9.4 per cent, respectively. The corresponding growth rates of world trade was about 5.7 per cent. The secular decline in India's share in world trade has been arrested and reversed, and the years ahead are likely to see a continuation of this increasing trend.

— The trade policy components of the reform process undertaken since July 1991 have been motivated by a full recognition of the important role that trade can play in promoting growth. The utilisation of the expanded scope for specialising in areas of comparative advantage is manifest in the improved growth performance of the economy. Furthermore, while exports have vigorously responded to the removal of the anti-export bias of a protectionist environment, domestic industry appears to have been stimulated by the expended availability of imported inputs and capital goods as well as the challenge of competing in the international market place. The positive response of Indian industry to liberalisation is amply demonstrated by the capital goods sector. The tariff on capital goods was as high as 85 per cent in the pre-reforms period. This has been reduced to about 25 per cent covering about 80 per cent of capital goods in 1995-96. The capital goods industry which witnessed a negative growth of 12.8 per cent in 1991-92, registered an average growth of about 23 per cent during 1994-96.

— The terms of trade, which measure the terms of exchange between a unit of exports and a unit of imports, have been improving in the post-reform period. Two common ways of measuring the terms of trade are the net terms of trade (NTT) and the income terms of trade (ITT). A time series indicating all parameters of terms of trade (TOT) for India since 1969-70 with the base of 1978-79 = 100 Indicates that there have been wide fluctuations in the TOT. The NIT (1978-79=100), which is an index of export prices divided by an index of import prices, improved from 109.3 in 1990-91 to 152.4 in 1994-95. It is

— It may be mentioned that India s purchasing power of exports as reflected thorough ITT has been improving continuously since 1985- 86. The value index of exports at 484 stands much higher than that of imports at 351 and hence, in terms of value, india has gained.But in terms of volume, the index of exports has been much less at 384 in comparison to that of imports at 515. This means that the volume of imports is increassing faster, though India is getting a better price for her exports.

— Compared to the experience of other developing countries, the improvement in the terms of trade for India has been very impressive. The NTT (1990=100), as presented in the UN's International trade Statistics Year Book, 1995, is reproduced below:

— Developing economies, with exports dominated by primary products, lost out to developed econoies,. Relavtive abundance of supply of primary products as well as the superior bargaining strength of developed countries have often ben adduced as two major reasons for the deterioration in the terms of trace. Gains in the terms of trade for India in the comparable period perhaps reflects her diversified export base as well as the relatively low international prices of oil in the relevant period.

India is committed to further liberalisation of its import regime, notwithstanding the dismantling of licensing controls over a wide area. At the same time, there are concerns whether developed nations of the world are implementing in letter and spirit their part of the obligations under the Uruguay Round Agreements. Many contries are resorting to protectinist devices in the guise of environmental hazards and exploitation of labour such as child labour. The obligations of providing access to imports of developing countries, especially textiles and garments, are being circumvented under one pretext or the other, even under the back-loaded integration of Textiles and Clothing into the World Trading System. Such restrictions are designed to keep out cheaper imports.

By virtue of the radical shift from a highly-regulated to an outward-oriented economy, India has attracted immense interest abroad, at both Governmental and private investor levels. India is one of the largest emerging markets, second only to China's, and the country has been experiencing inflows of foreign portfolio and direct investments—thought not as large as in China and a few other countries—which were unthinkable in the world of even 1980s. Economic strength has become the principal determinant of a nation's standing in the international community, and even the most powerful country, the United States of America, looks for market opportunities all over, more especially in the dynamic Asia-Pacific region, as the best shield of security.

With the end of the Cold War, the East-West barriers have broken down. The rapid spread of liberalisation and globalisation is a historic development which has blurred both East-West and North-South divisions. Developing countries have been compelled to adapt themselves to conditions of global interdependence although in the process they run grave risks in the medium-term and rare not assured of international safety nets.

In the rapidly changing world environment, each developing country must certainly concentrate on building its inherent strength and developing areas of comparative advantage and forge alliances with neighbours and, where promising, enter regional blocs which offer greater opportunities of trade and other exchanges to enhance national arena, disadvantaged nations must make common cause and unite to advance their pressing needs more effectively than what has been witnessed over the last fifty years in the post-decolonisation era. This is the only way of securing a post-cold war order which is just and equitable.

India has a long way to go before it could emerge as a strong global player, as currently it occupies the 32nd place as a leading exporter of merchandise, well below several countries in East and South-East Asia. It has to make up for the time lost in its inward-looking route to development which left the cuntry far behind in the international league, despite building a strong industrial base and possessing highly technical manpower, the third largest in the world. Indian planning did not take sufficient note of the gathering pace of global intergration with the frowth of merchandise trade exceeding the growth of output in virtually every year of the post-war period.

In recent years, India has begun to look East, is now a full dialogue partner in ASEAN (the 7-member Association of South East Nations) and excepts to find a place in the Asia Pacific Economic Forum (APEC) by 1999. These should promote greater intra-Asian trade and investment flows even as India strives to gain an increasing share of exports into developed economies of the West such as the European Union and North America. Trade with Russia and Eastern Europe as well as Central Asian States holds prospects of considerable expansion over present levels and a more promising development is the initiative taken by 14 states of the Indian Ocean Rim for an economic cooperation grouping with a Charter expected to be signed in March 1997.

The bilateral and pluralistic approaches cannot, and should not, in any way dilute India's firm commitment to multilaterialism which is the best safeguard against domination of the global economy by a few powerful nations. India's immediate responsibility is to solidify South Asian cooperation through SAPTA and ensure its early graduation to becomes SAFTA (South Asian Free Trade Area) to make it a region of good neighbourliness less prone to conflilcts than at present. With 16 per cent of the world's population, India's weight in the international economy remains negligible, and the building up of internal strength with determination through higher saving, and investments and greater efficiency in the use of resources is a pre-requisite for the country to claim its due share in the global market-place.

Looking Ahead

The fifth decade of Independence has triggered investment interest in India as never before. Policymakers should now bring in a lot more clarity on their objectives.

The rules of international trade have changed. Witrh trade barriers getting dismantled by the day, there is need to infuse a very high degree of competitiveness. A major development is the evolution of regional trade groupings like the European Community (EC), the North American Free Trade Association (NAFTA), ASEAN, APEC etc.

Though the south Asian countries have formed the SAARC, progress achieved in free trade among these has been slow. Apart from mere trade flows, potential benefits in terms of the phasing out of poliltical animosities and more cohesive regional developments are immense.... The EC experience proves this. Over the last 50 years Britain, France and Germany, who have been bitter adversaries for centuries, have been bonded together on the strength of mutuality of economic interests. The SAARC union could grow to include China, the Central Asian Republics and the Indian Ocean rim countries, including South Africa, and forge close links with ASEAN and APEC in course of time. The comparable levels of economic development of most of the countries in this region would help in co-ordinated growth.

There is a huge market for such equiptment: there are capabilities in these countries to produce entire range of such equipment–generators, turbines, boilers, transformers, switchgears, motors etc.

The Korean automobile manufacturers—Daewoo Motors and Hyundai—indicate plants for developing India as a major centre for their global operations. Like we did in regard to Maruti, in the assimilation of mass production technology, India should attempt absorption of the high productivity levels of the Koreans, Americans and others; combine this with the strength of the massive availability of skilled manpower to win global markets.

With the progress of economic reforms in many countries of the world and deregulation of financial markets, the importance of private capital flows into Asia has increased from US $ 76.8 billion in 1994 to US $ 98.0 billion in 1995, while net official flows increased marginally from US $ 5.6 billion to US $6.4 billlion during the same period. Similarly, while there were considerable official flows to Mexico and the transition countries in 1995 in support of their comprehensive adjustment programmes, net private capital flows to the developing countries increased from US $ 140.4 billion in 1994 to US $ 166.6 billion in 1995. India has has modest, but increasing, success in attracting a growing part of these private capital flows. Furthermore, much of these private capital inflows into India has been of the non-debt creating variety, and helped to boost the balance of payments as well as the availability of investible resources in the economy.

The international financial community is appreciative of India's economic performance in the last years, but concerns continue to be expressed about the high fiscal deficit, the slowing down of structural reforms, continued restrictions on consumer goods imports, and tariff levels considerably higher than in other countries. Also, references are often made to India's move towards capital account convertibility (with some observers advocating a cautions approach), high level of subsidies, inadequate disinvestment in the public sector, need for further relaxation of rules to attract foreign investment and the continued nigh stake of the government in the public sector banks. On the whole, the international community is very positive about India's effort to achieve a high rate of growth.

Participants in the India Development Forum (IDF) meeting in September 1996 acknowledged the strong performance of the Indian economy and appreciated the new Government's declaration to continue reform measures to strengthen the social programmes as set out in the Common Minimum Programme (CMP). Various delgates stressed the importance of (i) fiscal consolidation, (ii) sustaining programmes in the social sectors, (iii) infrastructrue, (iv) provety eradication, (v) reforms in agriculture, public sector, and financial sector, and (vi) strengthening of legislation against child labour. In support of India's economic development, the donor countries pledged official assistance in 1996-97 of US $ 6.7 billion. Inclusion of US $ 400 million in long-term finance, promised on a bilateral basis at market rates, will raise this total to above US $ 7 billion. About 33 per cent of the total could be in the form of grants and interest-free loans.

With effect from January 1, 1997, India subscribed to the Special Data Dissemination Standards (SDDS) of the

International Monetary Fund (IMF). by subscribing to the SDDS, India ha committed itself to streamilining the tatistical system of the country to produce most of the data categories with a much shorter time lag, improved quality and coverage by December 31, 1988.

By virtue of the radical shift from a highly-regulated to an outward-oriented economy, India has generated immense interest abroad, but it has a long way to go before emerging as a strong global player, opines the author. India's development strategy launched in the 1950s, soon after Independence, aimed mainly at strengthening the industrial base of the country, especially in basic goods and heavy machine-building, and adopted the import-substituation model to achieve self-reliance. Exports were not viewed as an integral part of overall economic development, and such imports as became unavoidable were financed by drawing down foreign exchange reserves that had accrued to India at the time of Independence, in the form of sterling balances held in its favour for goods and services provided by this country during the Second World War.

Export pessimism dominated the mood of the early planners as it was rightly assumed then that until India's manufactures began to be diversified, there was little possibility of exporting manufactures while primary products and traditional manufactured goods faced poor demand prospects in the world market. It was during the later half of the fifties, when the Second Five Year Plan was under way with its emphasis on heavy industry, largely in the public sector, that it began to be realised that India needed to export to be able to finance at least part of the maintenance and developmental imports.

The foreign exchange crisis that was looming by mid-1957 reinforced the importance of export growth as part of planned development. The pessimistic view about the potential for export earnings gave way to a more positive approach in the Third Plan (1961-66) with the introduction of export promotion measures without deflecting from the thrust of import subsitution and industrialisation. It was clear by mid-estimated the import content of the inward-looking path of development opted by India. Pressures on balance of pyaments had already brought into existence the Aid-India-Consortium comprising the World Bank and developed countries interested in providing assistance to India. Renewed emphasis on exports was laid in the Fourth Plan (1969-74) which envisaged porogressive elimination of dependence on foreign aid while the Fifth Plan (1974-79) identified certain sectors such as engineering goods, garments, leather manufacture and marine products for achieving increases in exports.

Thus, as agianst virtual stagnation in the 1950s, export performance improved to an average growth of 3 to 4 per cent in the 1960s, and was more impressive in 1970s with an average growth of 6.3 per cent in volume and 15.9 per cent in value terms.

But in the three decades, India's share in world exports had declined throughout from about 2 per cent in 1950 to 0.65 per cent in 1970 and dropped further to 0.42 per cent in 1980. This was the period when there was impressive growth in world trade and the opportunities were seize by many smaller Asian developing countries as well as the industrialising economies in Latin America to great advantage.

Paradoxically, even as india's export growth was being maintained or marginaly improved upon, her share of world exports was declining. Over the three decades ending the Seventies, the share of exports in Gross Domestic Product (GDP) ranged from 4 to 6 per cent. In a continental economy of India's size, the role of external sector in the development process was under-played so much that it took a successions of droughts, oil price shocks and balance of payments difficulties in the first two and a half decades of planning before the country could begin to see import substitution and export promotion as two sides of the same coin. But heavy reliance on quantitative restrictions on trade through import and export controls and detailed industrial licensing kept India a closed economy.

The Primary issuance of securities has a long history in India. The Indian bond market, measured by the estimated value of bonds outstanding, is next only to the Japanese and the Korean bond market in Asia. By January 31, 1995, the outstanding value of the Indian securities market was estimated to have reached Rs.3000 billion, almost 3.5 times its size in 1986. The size is deceptive as, despite attractive yields, secondary market trading has remained poor with virtually no quotation even in respect of listed securities. The estimated outstanding amount accounts for about 42% of GDP, as at the end of January 1995. Partial deregulation of interest rates in the early nineties and increasing emphasis on monetary policy in stabilization are the first major steps towards the emergence of an active debt market, with government securities spearheading the process. With the issuance of government securities at market determined coupon rates and the use of innnovative products, it has become possible, for the first time, for other issuers to offer debt products priced off the yield on government securities.

The process of financial sector reforms initiated in 1991, is far from complete. The Growth of the Indian Capital Market since Independence has been phenomenal. The number of stock exchanges increased from 7 in 1947 to 23 in 1994. Likewise the number of listed companies on stock exchanges grew from 1125 in 1946 to 7811 at the end of 994. Similarly, the quantum of listed capital registered a growth of about 565 times from Rs.270 crore in 1946 to Rs.152,322 crore at the end of March, 1994.

The basic objective of financial sector reforms is to promote a diversified, efficient and competitive financial system by a policy shift from detailed regulation and controls to one based on market forces. Alongwith dismantling administrative regulation, the goal is establishment of a system of prudential regulation, supported by a mechanism for reporting, monitoring and supervision of the compliance.

Another major plank of reform is injection of new competition into a hitherto virtually government owned financial system. For the first time in many years, six new banking licences have been granted to the private sector all of which have been implemented. The new banks are permitted to have financial joint ventures with fgoreign baks, particularly for accessing modern systems and technology. There has been a mushrooming of Non-Banming Finance Companies (NBFCs), some of whom have already built up a large net-work. Several well known investment banks have established a presence in India. Since April 1993, nearly 300 Foreign Institutional Inestors (FIIs) have been registered with the regulatory authority and quite a few are active investors in the domestic capital market which has been opened up to foreign portfolio investment in a limited way. Several new mutual funds have been set up by the private sector including some by global fund managers. The most spectacular growth has been registered when we compare the share of market capitalization to gross domestic products (GDP) which was 12.9% in 1946, while in 1991-92 it was 57.2% and further increased to 68.8% during 1993-98.

Trade policy

Side by side with the announcement of New Industrial Policy for Promoting Small Tiny and Village Enterprises, the Government have also announced major reforms in the Trade Policy. The main objective of the trade policy have been to progressively reduce the system of administrative controls and lilcences and to link import except in the case of essential items. The major reforms in the Trade Policy are given below:

Exports were in the past allowed replenishment to provide for essential inputs required for the manufacture of products exported. To allow flexibility to enable diversification of export products and also as an incentive for exports, the REP licenses so issued, were allowed to be freely sold. The entitlement for REP licenses also varied from item to item. In view of the flexibility of the REP Licenses Government realise that to treat it as licence is an misnomer, under the new policy the REP licences have been replaced by a new instrument named 'Eximscrips'. Eximscrips will be issued on the basis of FOB value of exports or Net FOreign Exchange (NFE) earnings from exports as indicated below. The main features of the new systems are:

The basic rate at which Eximscripts will be issued against exports will be 30% of FOB value. Exports to hard currency areas will be eligible for Eximscrips valid for hard currency imports while exports to rupee payment areas will be issued Eximscrips valid for imports from these areas only. However, as a measure of transition, exports to rupee payment areas may continue to avail of REP licences valid for hard currency imports at the rate prevailing prior to 4th July, 1991. This transition facility will be available only for exports effected upto 31st December 1991.

Products such as gems and jewellery, handcrafts, newspapers, journals and periodicals and cinematographic films, which enjoyed higher rated of REP will receive Eximscrips at the same rates as before.

The Basis rate of 30% is inadequate for exports of certain products such as value-added agricultural projects, electronics, bulk drugs and marine products, formulations and certain categories of advanced engineering goods. These products will be eligible for an additional Eximscrips entitlement of 10 percentage points, taking the total Eximscrips rate to 40% of FOB value.

For exports made on the basis of duty free imports obtained against Advance Licences, Eximscrips will be available at the general rate of 30% but this will be applied to the net foreign exchange earnings. On the same principle. Eximscrips at 30% of NFE will also be available for all EOU and EPZ units.

The 30% of NFE rate of Eximscrips is also applicable to service exports, including software exports which is a thrust area. The definition of services covered under this category is being ratinallized and extended to include other services such as services of architects, textile designers, artists, management consultants, lawyers etc. The benefit will be available to services exported by resident Indians for which remittances are made to India. The details are being notified separately.

Eximscrips issued to exporters will be tradeable and can be used to import any item in the limited permissible list (Appendix-3), the non-sensitive canalised list (Appendix-5A) and for all OGL, items for actual users (Appendix-6, List 8, Part I and List 10). Eximscrips earned by exporters on their own exports can also be used to import non-OGL capital goods other than those on the restricted list (Appendix-1A). All REP licences issued against exports prior to 4th July, 1991 will continue to be valid for the life of the licence and will have the same import entitlement as the new Eximscrips. Additional licences issued to export houses/trading houses, which were earlier valid for a more limited range of imports, will also be valid for the same range of imports as Eximscrips.

With the introduction of Eximscrips, the system of issuing supplementary licences of raw material, components and spares listed in Appendix-3 will be discontinued except for small scale industries and for manufacturers of specified life saving drugs and equipment. In future, all import requirements of these items (with the exceptions indicated above) will be made through Eximscrips, Similarly items in Appoendix-4 and Appendix-9, which were earlier importable against supplementary licences, will henceforth be importable only against Eximscrips. Import of items appearing in Appendix-2 Part B (list of Restricted Items) and Appendix-8 (List of Scientific and Measuring Instruments Restricted for Import) of the Import-Export Policy 1990-93 will continue to require licences. Such licences as well as licences required for small scale industries and manufactures of life saving drugs/equipment will be called Special Licences as these will be limited and include special cases.

As a measure of import compression and to strengthen the linkage between import capability and exports, two further changes have been made. The category of unlisted OGL has been abolished and these items have been shifted to Appendix-3. They are now importable only against Eximscrips (except for SSI and manufacturers of life saving drugs and equipment). In the case of units subject to the Phased Manufacturing

Programme (PMP), many of which benefit from concessional duty on their imports of OGL items, all such items will henceforth be importable only against Eximscrips.

Eximscrips will be issued only after export proceeds have been realised. The procedure for issue of Eximscrips has been streamlined and Government will ensure that Eximscrips are issued within 48 hours of the receipt of the application accompanied by single document, namely, the bank certificate for the realisation of export proceeds.

Advance Licences

The system of advance licences is designed to provide exporters with duty free access to the inputs they need to produce competitively for world markets. This is an important instrument of trade policy especially in our situation where tariff levels are still high. The Government has taken the following steps to strengthen the system of Advance Licences as an instrument of export promotion:

(i) The procedures for considering Advance Licence applications have been simplified to ensure that advance licences will be issued within 15 days of application in all cases where input-output norms have been fixed. Where norms have not been fixed, the licence will be issued within 45 days.

(ii) The number of documents accompanying an Advance licence application has been reduced from 9 to 3 where norms are prescribed and to 4 where they are not prescribed.

(iii) Ar present norms have been prescribed for 540 items. This will be increased to over 1000 items by 31st October, 1991 and more items will be covered thereafter.

(iv) Substantial Manufacturing Activity as a necessary condition under the Advance Licence Scheme will no longer be applicable for exports to the general currency area. However, the value addition norms will remain in force. A large number of exporters will benefit under this scheme.

(v) A new Scheme of Transferable Advance Licence has been introduced for GCA exports in selected thrust areas, namely textiles, leather goods and engineering industries. Under this scheme exporters can undertake exports based on duty paid inputs obtained from the market and subsequently obtain advance licences for replenishment of these inputs by duty free imports. These advance licences will be freely transferable. The coverage of the scheme will be extended on merits.

(vi) Advance licence will specify values in free foreign exchange both for the purpose of import and export. The currencies in which such values are denominated will be limited to those notified for this purpose by the RBI.

(vii) The Existing procedure for obtaining Bank Guarantee (BG) and Legal Undertaking (LUT) from different categories of exporters in being streamlined and liberalised as follows:

(a) Export/Trading/Star Trading House and Public Sector Undertakings will have the facility of obtaining advance licence against LUT only without any monetary limit.

(b) All manufacturing units having an annual turnover of at least Rs. 5 crores (including both domestic and exports turnover) during the previous 3 year would also be able to avail of the LUT facility up to a value limit of 50% of their annual production.

(c) A new unit without any production or export performance to its credit would also be allowed LUT facility provided it is promoted by an existing company with an annual production of Rs. 5 crores for more than three years. In such a case, both the new company and the promoting company would have to provide LUT.

(d) Bank guarantee and/or LUT obligation will be concurrent to the fulfilment of export obligation.

(viii) Exporters would be allowed to dispose of the materials imported against advance licences by way of replenishment without seeking prior permission of the licensing authority in cases where no MODVAT facility has been availed of on the domestic material used in exports.

(ix) Adjustment needed on account of fluctuation of prices of imported individual items would be permitted within the overall CIF value of advance licence.

(x) The power of revalidation which presently vests in the Licencing Committee at the Headquarters has been delegated to the Licensing Authorities.

(xi) In case where applications for an advance licence are turned down, the exporter will be permitted to convert to the Duty Drawback regime by the Collectors of Customs so that shipments made in advance can be imported on payment of duty subsequent claims of duty drawback.

(xii) Exporters can obtain advance release orders for domestic supply against advance licences under which the domestic supplier gets the benefit of deemed exports. Henceforth, release orders will be issued across the counter without requiring the name of the domestic supplier, which could be given later.

The adoption of these procedures would reduce discretionary controls and delays and afford much greater freedom to exporters in procuring essential duty free raw materials to maintain their competitiveness in the would market thereby promoting exports from the country.

The export Processing Zone scheme and the 100% EOU scheme were introduced to provide for duty-free enclaves, which would enable entrepreneurs to concentrate on production exclusively for export. However, with increasing liberalisation in the DTA, the duty advantages enjoyed by EPZs/EOUs have become less important. While the procedures of Customs Bonding are very onerous. The schemes have not therefore taken off as expected and they have also not attracted foreign investment aimed at tapping export markets to the extent that was expected. The working of these schemes has been reviewed and the following changes made:

(i) All EOUs/EPZ unit will be eligible for Eximscrips at the basic rate of 30% applied to net foreign exchange earning.

(ii) The duty applicable on DTA sales from EOUs/EPZ units is being reduced to 50% of the normal customs subject to the duty payable not being less than the excise duty on the same product. The extent of DTA sales allowed will be accordance with their entitlement. DTA sales will be permitted in the ratio of 25:75 in relation to export sales in case of units while use of indigenous raw material is more than 30% of production. In all other cases the ratio of permissible DTA sales to export sales will be 15:85. The procedures for clearing goods from the EOU/EPZ units for DTA sales are also being streamlined.

(iii) In order to encourage exporters to set up EOUs or

EPX units the net foreign exchange earned by EOUs or EPZ units can be clubbed with the earnings of their parent/associated companies in the DTA for the purpose of according Export House. Trading House of Star Trading House status for the latter.

(iv) The IPRS scheme for supply of steel to exporters will also be extended to EOUs and EPZ units. The Development Commissioners are being empowered to issue "payment authorities" in lieu of JCCI & Es.

Under the New Industrial Policy, most industries do not require an industrial licence except for a defined list. With a view to bringing about comparable streamlining in the procedure for EOU/EPZ approvals, a systems of automatic approvals is being established for all proposals which fall within certain parameters. Capital goods imports will be allowed under the automatic approvals procedure if they are fully covered by foreign equity or if they do not exceed 50% of the value of plant and equipment subject to a ceiling of Rs 3 crores. All proposals within the automatic approval parameters will be cleared within two weeks. All other proposals will be submitted to the Board of Approvals for consideration and decisions including issue of licences will be taken within 45 days.

A large number of issues relating to the operation of EOUs/EPZ units required centralized clearance in the Ministries of Commerce and Industry. Powers are being delegated to the Development Commissioners so that these approvals can be given on a decentralised basis. The specific approval of the Development Commissioner would not be required in cases of broad banding by EPZ units, where value addition is being maintained. The unit concerned would need only to provide relevant information to the Development Commissioner.

The following specific concessions to EOUs/EPZ units have also been extended:

(i) Allowing entry of imported raw material on "Provisional Assessment" basis, to expedite customs clearance.

(ii) Permitting units under the EPZ and EOU schemes to supply/transfer finished goods among themselves.

(iii) Replacement of multiple bond by a single bond, for obtaining import clearance.

(iv) Increasing the list of items under the "Special Imprest Licence Scheme" on selective basis.

(vi) Clarifying that containers stuffed in EPZ and EOUs are not to be reinspected at other points, as long as seals are intact.

Government have also decided to allow private parties to establish bonded warehouses within EPZs for stocking and sale of duty free raw materials, components, consumables and spares to EPZ units and EOUs. This will cut down delay in obtaining supplies of duty free materials which are in constant and regular demand by exporters. The details of this scheme will be notified shortly.

Other steps announced in the new Trade Policy have been the simplification of procedures for import of capital goods, decanalisation of number of items which were previously canalised, permission to allow established exporters to open foreign currency accounts in approved banks, raise external credits, pay for export related imports from such accounts and credit export proceeds to such accounts, its decision to re-designate the office of the Chief Controller of Import and Exports as Directorate General of International Trade with the principal function being to promote of exports, and facilitation of imports to promote export trade.

The policy changes now being implemented imply substantial reduction in the extent of licensing and in the number of types of licences. Supplementary licences for import of items in Appendixes-3 (except for SSI and manufacturers of life saving drugs and equipment), 4 and 9 of the Import-Export Policy 1990-93 have been abolished. Additional licences which were issued as an incentive to Export Houses and Trading Houses will stand abolished with effect from 1st April, 1992 and the incentive will take the form of an additional Eximscrip entitlement.

To achieve optimal import containment in the context of the present Balance of Payments situation, several steps have been taken. One of these is the shift of many items which are on OGL to the limited permissible list.

With these changes, the policy for import of raw materials components and other inputs needed for production has been simplified. Most raw materials and other inputs (except for those on the Restricted List) can be freely imported either against Eximscrips or on OGL. Some raw materials continue to be canalised but in more of these cases requirements beyond those provided by the canalising agencies can be met through Eximscrips.It is the policy of the Government to move to a situation where imports of essential raw materials and components needed for industrial production are regulated through appropriate tariffs. However, in view of the Balance of Payments position which necessitates continued import containment, this cannot be done immediately. Many items must therefore remain on the limited permissible list, with imports permitted only against Eximscrips.

The medium term objective of the Government is to progressively eliminate licensing and quantitative restrictions on capital goods and raw materials/

components so that all these items can be placed on OGL save for a small carefully defined negative list. This shift is proposed to be achieved over a 3 to 5 year period. The Government will appoint a High Level Committee to work out the modalities of achieving this transition keeping in mind the Balance of Payments position and the need to rationalise the reduce tariffs progressively to provide Indian Industry with an appropriate environment to develop international competitiveness.

Industrial Policy and Trade Policy of the Government of India

Over the years the Government of India has been adopting various measures for the liberalisation of the Industrial Policy, for streamling the licensing and foreign collaboration procedures, for reducing the number of agencies which the prospective investors have to approach to get the necessary approvals, etc., with the objective of attracting more investment and technology transfer. On the 24th July, 1991 the Government tabled before Parliament the Statement on Industrial Policy, 1991, which was followed by the issuance of a Notification by the Department of the Industrial Development to implement the Policy Statement and a series of Press Notes to set out the changes in the existing system and procedure for obtaining industrial licenses and approval of proposals for foreign and for foreign testing of indigenous raw materials and products and indigenously developed technlogies.

The new Industrial Licensing Policy of the Government of India has exempted form the requirement of obtaining industrial licence all industries, except those reserved for the Public Sector (Schedule I to the the Notification), those in respect of which Idustrial Licensing is compulsory (Schedule II to the Notification) and those relating to the items reserved for exclusive manufacture in the small scale sector (Schedule III to the Notification).

The exemption from Industrial licensing is also subject to:

The proposed project (except in the case of a project relating to electronics, computer software, printing industry, industry located within an area designated as 'industrial area' by a State Government before the 25th July, 1991 or the small scale or the ancillary sector) being not located with 25 kilo meters form the periphery of the standard urban area limits of a city having a population of more than one million according to the 1991 census; and of the Central and the State environmental laws and regulations including local zoning and land use laws and regulations.

Units qualifying for exemption from industrial licensing in accordance with the foregoing conditions are required only to file a Memorandum in the prescribed form, before establishement of the project, with the Department of Industrial Development (Secretariat for Industrial Approvals) together with a crossed demand draft for rupees one thousand in favour of the Pay and Account Officer, Department of Industrial Development and another Memorandum in the prescribed form at the time of commencement of commercial production.

Small scale and ancillary units are required, as before, to be registered with the Director of Industries of the concerned State. Manufacturing units with an investment in plant and machinery up to Rs. 60 lakhs, ancillary units with an investment in plant and machinery up to Rs. 75 lakhs and units which are willing to undertake an export obligation to the extend of 30 per cent of their annual production by the third year with an investment up to Rs. 75 lakhs are eligible for small scale registration.

The new industrial policy of the Government of India has announced major liberalisation for attracting foreign investment in respect of a list of high priority industries. Foreign equity investment up to 51 per cent will be allowed subject only to the condition that;

— The requirement of imported capital goods should be covered by the foreign equity;

— The amount of dividend payment may be converted by export earnings of such items recorded in Years prior to the payment of dividend or in the year of payment of dividend. This will be monitored by the Reserve Bank of India. However, such balancing will not be required beyond a period of seven years from commencement of production.

In all such cases the Reserve Bank of India has been authorised to issue automatic approvals of foreign investment and also grant exemption from the operation of the relevant sections of the Foreign Exchange Regulations Act, 1973.

Milestones

1962
Indian National Committee for Space Research (INCOSPAR) formed by the Department of Atomic Energy and work on establishing Thumba Equatorial Rocket Launching Station (TERLS) started.

1975-76
Satellite Instructional Television Experiment (SITE) conducted.

1977
Satellite Telecommunication Experiments Project (STEP) carried out.

1979
Bhaskara-I, an experimental satellite for earth observations, launched (June 7,1979).

1993

INSAT-213, the second satellite in the INSAT-2 series, launched (July 23,1993).

First developmental launch of PSLV with IRS-1E on board (September 20, 1993). Satellite could not be placed in orbit.

1994

Fourth developmental launch of ASLV with SROSS-C2 on board (May 4, 1994). Satellite placed in orbit.

Second developmental launch of PSLV with IRS-P2 on board (October 15, 1994). Satellite successfully placed in polar sunsynchronous orbit.

1996

Third developmental launch of PSLV with IRS-P3 on board (March 21, 1996). Satellite placed in polar sunsynchronous orbit.

1997

INSAT-2D, fourth satellite in the INSAT series, launched (June 4,1997). Becomes inoperable on October 4, 1997. (An in-orbit satellite, ARABSAT-1C, since renamed INSAT-213T, was acquired in November 1997 to partly augment the INSAT system).

First operational launch of PSLV with IRS-1D on board (September 29, 1997). Satellite placed in orbit.

1998

INSAT system capacity augmented with the readiness of INSAT-2DT acquired from ARABSAT (January 1998).

Liquid propulsion strap-on stage of GSLV successfully qualified (March 5,1998).

First flight cryogenic stage of GSLV received from Russia (September 20,1998).

6

Sponsored Research

Sponsored Research Programme (RESPOND) under which Department of Space supports research, educational and scientific activities at academic institutions, is an important element of the Space-Academic interaction. The support under repond include projects in space science, application and technology, support to Space Technology Cells (STC), space science and education cells, conferences and symposia, publications and other scientific activities of relevance to space programme. The R and D programmes and STC programmes are reviewed by DOS centres and the project results directly utilised for space programmes. Respond has thus strengthened the interaction between DOS and academic institutions and has also enabled in training students, teachers and scientists working in the academic institutions by carrying out space research activities.

During the year, six projects supported at the academic institutions, have been completed. They are related to nozzle flows, problems of pollution in estuarine systems diffusion bonded titanium alloys and stainless steel, development of gelled monomethyl hydrazine propellants, investigations of buildings under acoustic loads and development of $LiNbO_3$ substrates for Surface Acoustic Wave (SAW) devices.

Twenty new projects in 16 academic institutions

have been initiated during the year. They include: Studies on solar convection and oscillations, quasi periodic oscillations of Black hole candidates, analysis of rotor dynamic performance of cryogenic engine turbopumps, identification of sources of coal and conditions to obtain tar application in carbon fibres, vibro-acoustic analysis of launch vehicle structures using statistical energy, ultrasonic pulse echo detection system for measurement of burning rate, electro-chemical joining of dissimilar metals, development of fuzzy techniques and genetic logarithms for control systems, theoretical and experimental investigation of composites, payload recovery simulation, electrochemical preparation of dinitrogen pentoxide, improving properties of important al-alloys through trace-addition, development of integrated system software for launch vehicles and transonic dynamics, of use of IRS data for updating of maps classification of urban features and management of rural road networks, hydrological assessment and simulation, image processing techniques for improved wind estimation using INSAT cloud and water vapour data and studies on interplay of source and channel code parameters in digital satellite communications.

Space Technology Cells (STC) have been set up in some institutions to carry out research activities. The projects in these STC's include study of monsoon cloud systems using high resolution satellite imagery, development of absorption cryocooler, synthesis and characterisation of nanoparticles of Ni and Ni-Pd alloys, development of a finite-volume-based procedure for computing radiative heat flux in spacecraft, water balance and evapotranspiration studies using remote sensing, growth of In-Sb based epilayers for infrared detector applications, development of polyphosphazenes-heat resistant polymers for space applications, studies of mechanics of interface fracture in layered solids, development of upwind algorithms for real-gasflows inequilibrium and chemical nonequilibrium and electron spin resonance studies of irradiation effects in polymers and glasses, application of electron beam welding techniques on titanium alloys, statistical energy analysis of acoustic response of launch vehicle structures, development and testing of two-dimensional supersonic combustion, studies on the interaction between multiple supersonic jets, analysis of air-breathing vehicles modelling of the three-dimensional unsteady/ steady state compressible, flows, aero-elastic studies on aerospace materials, study of topography and earth crust movement using radar interferometry development of cryo-coolers for spacecraft, digital compression of remotely sensing images, slosh studies, fibre-matrix interface matrix composites, study of radiation-hardened CMOS process, analysis of stereo images from IRS digital elevation models, use of linear matrix inequalities in satellite control, thermomechanical analysis of 3d composites, generation of non-linear, development of fuzzy control for flexible structures and analysis of high resolution urban scenes from IRS satellites.

Space science and educational cells have also been established in the Indian universities. Research related to determination of moisture in rocket motors, development of smart fibre optic sensors, study of irradiation effects of MeV energy electrons on semiconductor devices and plastic materials, have been initiated. Students and Scientists from the universities also carry out research activities in atmospheric physics using MST Radar facility at Tirupati.

During this year DOS supported 32 conference and symposia in important areas of space science and technology and ten publication activities.

7

Space Industry Partnership

Since the inception of Indian space programme partnership with industry has been identified as a key area. With careful nurturing, this partnership has matured into a rewarding relationship. With the objectives of achieving self-reliance, active participation from Indian industries in the execution of space projects has been sought and considerable importance given in initiating and strengthening cooperative ventures with industries through know-how transfers, provision of technological consultancy and utilisation of industrial capability through and farming out fabrication contracts procurement of material. So far 231 technologies have been transferred to industries and 180 consultancy projects have been undertaken for the industries. Over 500 small, medium and large scale industries are involved in partnership with space.

Technology transfer

During the year, know-how for rapid thread checking machine technology has been transferred to industry. Industries have been identified for transfer of technologies such as automated tensile testing machine, conformal coating unit, polyimide film casting etc. A number of technologies and application software packages related to vibration isolators, sodium silicate metal-vulcanised rubber bonding adhesive pico ammeter, RF powermeter interface, Surface Acoustic Wave filters and delay lines, microwave band pass filters, microwave passive components, RS-232 fibre optic extender, PC based antenna controller, foldable umbrella antenna, automatic frequency control system, RF power meter interface, Ku-band feed high power amplifier, extended C-band offset feed antenna, etc., are in the pipeline for transfer to industry.

High technology ingredients for solid and liquid propellants and spacecraft propulsion system, materials, such as carbon cloth, etc., are being produced by industries under licence.

Front-end processing hardware and low cost real-time data acquisition system f or IRS-P3 satellite have been supplied by licensee industries to different users and also installed at IRS data reception stations, in DLR-Germany. Pressure transducers and temperature probes have been successfully qualified by the licensee industries for buy-back of these items for space projects. Fabrication of microwave invar filters has also progressed well during the year. It is proposed to use industries for machining and supplying of cavity and iris components for INSAT-3A communication payload. Qualification of vacuum brazing operations is in progress. Vibration and signal processing units are being supplied by industries after their successful test-and evaluation.

Patents and copyrights

During the year, three applications for patent have been filed and three patents granted. These include an improved process of gold plating on Magnesium alloys substrates, a process of black anodising on magnesium alloys, a process of black chromate coating on magnesium-aluminium alloys. Application has been made for copyright on "Geoimage software". Patent awareness workshops are being conducted with a view to make DOS scientists and engineers "Patent conscious" and spreading the patent culture.

Technological consultancy

Technological consultancy covering mechanical, electrical, electronics and chemicals fields is being provided to various industries. More than 180 consultancy assignments have been undertaken so far. During the year, seven consultancy assignments, including baseline mapping of Gir protected area, acreage- estimation of mentha crop in parts of Uttar Pradesh and Punjab, preparation of development plan for Pimpri-Chinchwad Municipal Corporation using remote sensing and GIS technologies and development of automobile HMCs, have been undertaken. Several assignments on training, testing and qualification of hardware and subsystems from industries and other Research and Development institutions have also been taken up.

Good progress has been made on the consultancy agreements signed in the previous years. Urban area mapping for Gujarat Infrastructure Ltd., Ahmedabad, and tree clad area mapping for Sardar Sarovar Narmada Nigam Ltd., Gandhinagar have been completed. An interim report of Gir Protected Area showing vegetation status, biodiversity rich zone and forest fire status has already been prepared and acreage estimation of Mentha crop for Everest Flavours, Ltd. completed. Development of Data Broadcast Service has been completed and demonstrated to customers.

Market survey and system studies

Prominent market survey and system studies assignments that were taken up during the year include those for Doppler Weather Radar System and remote sensing applications using IRS-1C/11) data. Studies on Digital Satellite Broadcasting service and an in-depth analysis on commercialisation of remote sensing have also been carried out. The results of these surveys have provided valuable inputs towards technology transfer efforts.

Technology utilisation

Indian industries continue to support all important space projects, like PSLV, GSLV, IRS and INSAT, through development and fabrication of hardware and building of development and testing infrastructure. Industries have been involved in the fabrication of a variety of hardware, structural subassemblies, light alloy structures, thermal control systems for satellites, solid state power amplifiers for spacecraft payload, propellants, etc. In certain cases, industries have also augmented their facilities to suit. growing needs of space programme in terms of development and fabrication of specialised products and processes. Industry participation has been increasing, especially in the areas of precision machining, precision assembly, fabrication and integration of electronic packages, critical components for inertial systems and liquid engines. Many of the flight electronics parts and subsystems, avionics packages including on-board telemetry, telecommand and communication packages, are being produced by the industries. A Memorandum of Understanding has been signed with an industry for the fabrication of space quality solar panels.

Fabrication of Mobile Satellite Service (MSS) reporting terminal and digital sound and data broadcast receivers has been taken up by selected industries. First batch of these units have been delivered for qualification. Fabrication of antennas reflectors, feeds, mounts, racks, boxes, helical filters, co-axial attenuators, SMA connectors, PCBs, etc., have been carried out at various work centres.

Export promotion

Antrix Corporation Limited, the commercial arm of Department of Space, has undertaken a number of export initiatives for space products and services. Antrix has continued to expand its market base and there has been an increased quantum of revenues accrued during the year.

One of the major activities of Antrix is to promote a wider usage of remote sensing data from IRS satellites. In association with a US company, efforts are being pursued towards this end. The network of international ground stations set up to receive, process and market IRS data products in different countries is now expanding. Six international ground stations - Norman in USA, Neustralitz in Germany, Bangkok in Thailand, Japan, Dubai and Korea - have been upgraded to receive IRS data. Antrix has also supplied the required hardware and software for IRS data reception. Additional ground stations in Australia and Saudi Arabia, are in various stages of completion for receiving IRS data. Proposals for more IRS reception stations at Alaska and Equador are getting ready. As many as ten ground stations around the globe are expected to receive IRS data in due course.

Supply of satellite hardware to companies overseas including pressure transducers and fill and drain valves, has been undertaken. The contracts for these supplies called for stringent space quality requirements and tight delivery schedules which have been successfully met. Some more hardware like solar wing actuators and hinge assemblies and magnetic torquer rods are in the various stages of fabrication. Execution of these orders have benefited the space programme while meeting requirement of international standards. Technical and consultancy services are also being offered to Electronics and Telecommunications Research Institute (ETRI), Korea, for their spacecraft mission control system.

During the year, telemetry, command and ranging station along with S-band support for on-orbit control of Afristar (one of the three satellites of WorldSpace), has been established in Bangalore. Afristar has been launched and the station is now in operation. Satellite mission support activities are steadily growing through existing and new customers. Antrix has also executed a contract with PanAmsat for providing TTC services to PAS-7 and with Space Systems Loral, USA for TTC services and in-orbit test support for their satellite.

The market for telecommunication satellite for private sector service providers is also being tapped by Antrix. A contract has been signed with an Indian company for providing consultancy services for its satellite project aimed at owning and launching a satellite as an Indian registered satellite system. Negotiations are underway for marketing of telecommunication satellites jointly with leading spacecraft manufacturers.

A beginning has been made in the area of launch vehicles services too. Antrix has entered into agreements with Satellite Technology Research Centre of the Republic of Korea for the launch of their small satellite (KITSAT-3) weighing about 100 kg and with German Aerospace Center (DLR) for the launch of its small satellite, TUBSAT, weighing about 50 kg. Both these satellites would be launched as piggybacks to Indian Remote Sensing satellite, IRS-P4, on board PSLV-C2. Antrix has also signed an agreement with VERHAERT Design & Development N.V, Belgium for launching its micro satellite, PROBA, weighing about 100 kg as an auxiliary payload on-board a forthcoming PSLV flight. A Memorandum of Understanding has also been reached with Arianespace, France for evolving a common launch vehicle interface for small satellites.

8

Cooperation

Execution of space programme entails cooperation with a number of academic and research institutions, industries, the end users and space agencies in other countries. INSAT system which is a joint venture of the Department of Space, Department of Telecommunications, India Meteorological Department, All India Radio and Doordarshan, is coordinated by Secretaries level INSAT Coordination Committee. National Natural Resources Management System (NNRMS) has the participation of a number of Central and State departments. NNRMS is guided by the Planning Committee of NNRMS with Member (Science), Planning Commission as Chairman. Space science activities are overseen and guided by the Advisory Committee on Space Sciences (ADCOS). Geosphere-Biosphere Programme is being undertaken in coordination with a number of scientific institutions in the country. Details of participation of academic and research institutions and industries in the space programme have already been covered in previous chapters.

International cooperation

Indian space programme, since its inception, has pursued international cooperation very actively. The establishment of Thumba Equatorial Rocket Launching Station, conduct of SITE and STEP, launches of Aryabhata, Bhaskara-I and Bhaskara-II, IRS-1A, IRS-1B and APPLE, manned space mission, development of Vikas engine for PSLV second stage, etc., involved active cooperation with other space agencies/countries. India has flown payloads of other space agencies on its sounding rockets. The Modular Opto-electronic Scanner developed by the German space agency, DLR, was included as one of the payloads on board Indian Remote Sensing satellite, IRS-P3, and the payload is sending valuable ocean-related scientific data. Details of international cooperation activities during the year are covered in the following paragraphs.

Brunei

Following an agreement with the Government of Brunei, Darussalam, a telemetry, tracking and telecommand station for satellites and launch vehicles is being set up in Brunei.

Canada

Under Memorandum of Understanding with the Canadian Space Agency (CSA), cooperative programmes in different aspects of space science, technology and applications, including commercial tie ups, are being considered.

China

Cooperation is being pursued with China National Space Administration (CNSA) in the areas of space science, technology and applications.

European Space Agency (ESA)

Under an agreement with the European Space Agency, several areas of cooperation have been identified making use of each other's expertise and facilities. Microwave remote sensing data from the synthetic aperture radar on board ERS satellites is being acquired regularly in India. Cooperation in studies relating to definition of navigation satellite systems for air traffic control is also being pursued. India participated in the Euro-Asia Space Week organised by ESA during the year in Singapore.

France

An Agreement has been signed with the French Space Agency, CNES on cooperation in peaceful uses of outer space between the two agencies. A specific agreement has also been signed for cooperation in satellite network operations. Preliminary studies on a joint satellite mission known as Megha-Tropiques for obtaining research data on tropical convective systems is being jointly carried out. Cooperation in the field of remote sensing training, promotion of value added services in remote sensing, flight opportunities for CNES experiments on IRS satellites etc., are also being considered.

Germany

Under a Special Arrangement between the German Aerospace Research Establishment (DLR), several areas of cooperation of mutual interest are being pursued. Indian scientists and engineers are taking part in several joint development efforts in DLR centres under this arrangement. Areas of cooperation include processing of synthetic aperture radar data analysis of stereoscopic remote sensing data, artificial intelligence for satellite operations, orbit determination, structural analysis and a few areas of space science. Data from the Modular Opto-electronic Scanner (MOS) of DLR flown on board IRS-P3 satellite is being analysed by scientists from India and Germany as well as by scientists in other parts of the world.

Three sounding rocket flights were carried out from Sriharikota during the year, with German instruments on board, for the study of ionosphere. A workshop on applications of synthetic aperture radar was held at Bangalore as part of the cooperative programme in which several scientists from both countries participated.

Hungary

India has signed an agreement with Hungarian Space Office for cooperation in the exploration and utilisation of outer space for peaceful purposes. A delegation from Hungary visited some of the Space Centres during the year in pursuance of this agreement.

Indonesia

As per a Memorandum of Understanding with National Institute of Aeronautics and Space (LAPAN) of the Republic of Indonesia, establishment of telemetry, tracking and command station for satellites and launch vehicles has been set up there.

Japan

A joint space panel for establishing and carrying out scientific and technological cooperation under the umbrella of an agreement between India and Japan is under consideration.

Mauritius

India has set up a TTC station at Mauritius to support IRS mission. The station also provides support for the initial tracking of PSLV using Precision Coherent Monopulse C-band (PCMC) Radar System set up there by India. A remote sensing centre and a satellite meteorology station have been set up in Mauritius with assistance from India.

Norway

Under an MOU with the Norwegian Space Centre, a test flight of an Indian sounding rocket has been carried out from Norway. Cooperation in the area of satellite tracking is also under consideration.

Peru

An MOU for cooperation in space has been signed with the National Space Agency of Peru (CONIDA). Several areas of space research are under consideration for taking up co-operative activities.

Russia

Agreements have been signed with Russia for cooperation in the peaceful uses of outer space. A Joint Working Group, under the agreement, has identified specific areas for scientific cooperation.

Sweden

Under the frame-work of a Memorandum of Understanding with Swedish Board of Space Activities (SBSA), a collaborative project with Swedish Royal Institute of Technology on the management of water resources for irrigated areas, with geographical information system, has made significant progress during the year.

Syria

A Memorandum of Understanding has been signed with General Organisation for Remote Sensing in Syria for cooperation in remote sensing applications. A pilot project for remote sensing applications in a ' Syrian site is being carried out with technical and scientific assistance from India.

The Netherlands

Post-graduate diploma courses on human settlement analysis are being conducted routinely at Indian Institute of Remote Sensing (IIRS), Dehradun, as part of a collaboration programme with ITC of The Netherlands. Increased cooperation between ITC and IIRS is also being considered.

Ukraine

An Agreement has been signed between India and Ukraine for cooperation in peaceful uses of outer space. Several possibilities for cooperative programmes are being examined by both sides.

United Kingdom

Under a Memorandum of Understanding with British National Space Centre (BNSC) for cooperation in space, several companies from both countries have been brought together for discussion on joint ventures in several areas.

United States of America

An MOU has been signed between India's Department of Space and the Department of Science and Technology (DST) and the US National Aeronautics and Space Administration (NASA) and National Oceanic and Atmospheric Administration (NOAA) for cooperation in the area of earth and atmospheric sciences. This involves carrying out joint research projects with exchange of visits and satellite data from both sides. Another MOU has been signed among ISRO, the German Aerospace Centre (DLR) and NASA for reception of data from DLRs Modular Opto-electronic Scanner instrument on ISRO's IRS-P3 satellite, at NASA's ground station for carrying out ocean related studies.

COSPAS-SARSAT system

India, as a member of the international COSPAS-SARSAT programme, has set up Local User Terminal (LUT) and Mission Control Centre (MCC) at Bangalore and LUT at Lucknow as part of Low Earth Orbiting Satellite Search and Rescue (LEOSAR) network. Indian MCC/LUTs provide real time coverage to a large part of Indian Ocean area covering Bangladesh, Bhutan, Kenya, Maldives, Nepal, Seychelles, Somalia, Sri Lanka, Tanzania, Thailand and Zanzibar. India has also flown search and rescue transponders on board INSAT satellites to complement low earth orbit satellite system.

General

India is playing a very active role in the UN Committee on Peaceful Uses of Outer Space (UN-COPUOS) and the International Astronautical Federation (IAF). India holds the Chairmanship of the United Nations Committee on Peaceful Uses of Outer Space (UN-COPUOS). DOS continues to participate in the technical activities of the inter-space agency, SFCG which is an informal forum for all space agencies to discuss frequency coordination related issues.

India, Chairman of the international Committee on Earth Observation Satellites (CEOS), hosted the Secretariat and steered the CEOS activities till November 1998. The 12th Plenary was hosted by India in November 1998 at Bangalore. An international symposium on Earth Observation for Sustainable Development was organised in India by the International Society for Photogrammetry and-Remote Sensing in February 1998. India will be hosting the second ESCAP Ministerial Conference on Space Applications in New Delhi during December 1999.

India actively participates in international science campaigns like Geosphere-Biosphere Programme and Indian Ocean Experiments (INDOEX). DOS has an active role in the Inter Agency Space Debris Coordination Committee (IADC), International Space University (ISU), Asian Association for Remote Sensing (AARS), Committee on Space Research (COSPAR), UN-ESCAP, etc. Several personnel from developing countries have been trained in India, specifically in the area of space-based remote sensing applications, under SHARES (Sharing of Experience in Space) scheme of DOS.

Centre for Space Science and Technology Education in Asia Pacific (CSSTE-AP)

The Centre for Space Science and Technology Education in Asia Pacific (CSSTE-AP), has been established by India at the initiative of the United Nations and is administered by an International Governing Board with representatives from Asia Pacific countries and United Nations. CSSTE-AP has been set up around the facilities of the Indian Institute of Remote Sensing (IIRS), Dehradun and the Space Applications Centre (SAC), Ahmedabad, of the Department of Space.

The Centre offers Post-Graduate education courses, leading to award of M Tech/ MSc (Tech) degrees in Remote Sensing and Geographical Information Systems, Satellite Communications, Satellite Meteorology and Space Sciences to students of different countries in the region. Since its establishment in 1995, CSSTE-AP has already conducted two 9-month courses on Remote Sensing and GIS, one on Satellite Communications and one on satellite meteorology. The third course on Remote Sensing and GIS has started in October 1998 with 22 students from 11 countries participating in the course.

Broadcast media

There is pressure to preserve history and to advance knowledge by storing information in some from that will enable succeeding generations to begin with the society's accumulated knowledge and experience. Thus, the culture is able to survive and make advances that will improve the lives of all its members. Early records were kept by forming tablets of dried mud and straw, then carving symbols in these panels so that information could be recalled. As anyone who has carried a heavy book bag across campus can imagine, clay tablet had the advantage of permanency, but they were hardly portable or convenient to use.

By 2000 B.C., it the ancient cultures of Egypt, Rome, and Greece, scrolls that could be rolled up and stored conveniently were in use. Papyrus plants were made into watery pulp, pressed into long rolls, dried, and then inscribed with hand-written symbols. Scrolls allowed records to be preserved, laws to be set down, and proclamations to be issued for rereading throughout the land.

In the first century A.D., parchment began to replace papyrus. The use of animal materials made possible folding and stitching of the writing surface, thus making rudimentary bound books with heavy wooden covers possible for the first time. The Chinese used a combination of vegetable materials including bark, rags, and husks to make the first true papers for artistic purposes. The making of paper spread to Europe during the Middle Ages, where it was used by monks to inscribe Biblical material. Handwritten books became available to the very rich, but the arduous task of copying precluded wide dissemination of written material.

Although the Chinese were engaged in printing before Johann Gutenberg's first efforts in 1450, Gutenberg is associated with "invention" of printing because he brought the various printing technologies together in a way that made quality reproduction of books and pamphlets possible with greater speed and lower cost. In his shop in Mains, Germany, Gutenberg adapted the wine press, which had a giant screw that could be tightened gradually down against a flat surface. Instead of pressing grapes into wine, he pressed sheets of paper against ranks of raised movable type arranged in works and locked into a flatbed from.

Gutenberg's technique prevailed for centuries. Even after the evolution of high-speed rotary presses and, still later, electronic photo-offset techniques that rendered raised metal printing obsolete, Gutenberg's basic concepts survived. Today some specialized printing is still performed on flatbed presses modeled after Gutenberg's. Gutenberg died a personal failure, and his son-in-low-Johann Fust actually carried out the printing operations that made Gutenberg famous. That printing operation ignited the imagination of others, who set up similar presses and gave birth to the craft of printing in Europe. Guilds of craftsmen controlled production in the mid-fifteenth century, and the acceptance of printing as a recognised craft was another step in the printing "revolution."

Printing "Revolution"

The term revolution suggests that the basic functions of society are changed radically. This can be accomplished when one faction overthrows another and institutes a new social order. However, revelations can occur without bloodshed and without the obvious overthrowing of established order. Such revolutions occur when innovation explodes, captures the fancy of the masses, and reworks the fundamental ways that society receives, distributes, and processes information.

Such a revolution occurred when printing in common language were available throughout Europe. Literate people, whose numbers were growing, could read material that was not controlled by the state or church or available only to the learned. The availability of such information created a greater demand for it. And the ability of the masses to "read for themselves" instead of being informed by priests, academics, or lords meant that individuals could make interpretations and rise questions on their own. Society thus was reshaped.

Today we understand that information can fuel revolution. But when printing was first introduced, no one could understand what changes it would work on society. An Englishman, William Caxton, learned from the European craftsmen and set up his country's first printing press in 1476. Caxton is credited with printing the first books in English, but he did so only at the pleasure of the rulers and the patronage of the wealthy. They wished to see Caxton's press bring the literature, and thus the culture, of other lands to England. However, they feared that an unrestrained printer also could bring new ideas hostile to the current from of government.

Thus, as printing spread in England, it was carefully controlled. Henry VIII had time between his may courtships to ban the publication of books not on an approved list, including most foreign titles. Eventually the Stationer's Company was organized to license and control publishers, and the Star Chamber Court was instituted to punish those defied the orders. Not until a general revolution broke out in 1640 did publishers routinely begin to defy the ever-changing laws regulating written expression. The first printing press to cross the Atlantic went not to the British Colonies, but to Mexico City, where the Spanish archbishop authorized the printing of religious works beginning in 1539.

A mere 20 years after the Pilgrims landed in the Colonies, bringing their Bibles with them, the first printing press at Harvard College in Cambridge, Massachusetts, was used to publish Bay Psalm Book: The Whole Books of Psalms in 1640. The audience for books was limited by common illiteracy, the small size of the colonial population, and little leisure time among the first settlers. Thus the press was used primarily for publishing folios, 16-page pamphlets, many of which could be assembled by the reader into a cumulative collection not unlike the Time-Life Library series so popular today.

Early publishers, conceded in Boston, Philadelphia and New York were not concerned with the masses, who had neither the education nor the money for books. The cultured few-in elect, the colonial aristocracy—were avid collectors of books from Europe as well as the new land. But local government, controlled by the landowners, placed restriction on the distribution of books. The laboring class was not encouraged to read, nor were many of the settlers who pushed westward. It was more than a century after the first press was in operation the books finally became popular medium in the United States of America.

Shorter publications—neither newspapers nor magazines, yet hardly substantial enough to put been hard covers—were created and few an appetite for information even in colonial days. The most celebrated of these was Benjamin Franklin's Poor Richard's Almanac, a compendium of planting information, wise sayings, quips, commonsense health tips, tide tables, and comments on manners and morals. Franklin's almanac appeared in the 1730s and was published annually of a quarter-century. By then other almanacs had appeared. Many were published for profit by printers, and many more were given away or sold at low cost by merchants and manufactures who used the publications to advertise their wares.

Franklin is credited with establishing the first subscription library scheme. As we shall see, this most ingenious of our founding fathers was instrumental in the development of book publishing that spurred reading in the new land, as well as a pioneer in newspapering and publication of the forerunners of the magazine.

Indisputably the best book collection in early America was assembled by Thomas Jefferson—a collection that provided the foundation for the Library of Congress. As America grew, education was put at a premium, and the new school systems created new readers. Cities began to provide more services for their citizens, including free libraries. Book reading and publishing began to surge.

By the 1850s, books were being written by American authors for consumption by a mass audience. Among the most popular were the dime novels, which literally sold for 10 cents, a few hours' pay for a laborer. The "Luck and Pluck" series written by Horatio Alter, Jr. in the 1870s like his earlier "Ragged Disk" and "Tattered Tom" series, appealed to recent immigrants who longed to pull themselves up by their bootstraps in the land of opportunity. Alger and other popular authors extolled the virtues of hard work, honesty, and willingness, to try again in the face of adversity. Thus they gave shape to a uniquely American value system. Around the middle of the century, textbook publishing was spurred by the success of the McGuffey Eclectic Readers. Also during this period the American novel come into its own with the publication of such classics as The Scarlet Letter by Nathaniel Hawthorn and Moby Dick by Herman Melville, ending a dependence on Europe for quality fiction.

The Civil War spurred book production because there was a great demand for reading material from the troops, who spent months and years far from home, often with little to do except read. Wars often have a profound effect on publishing because of the hunger for new information from those who have seen new places and things, and the intriguing subject matter created by conflict and human misery. After the Civil War, paperback books, many publish as a sideline by metropolitan newspapers, became extremely accessible to the mass audience; their low cost was due in large part to the fact that American publishers were reproducing European classics and new titles without paying any royalties (compensation to the authors). An international copyright law requiring the payment of royalties ended the first heyday of the paperback for a half-century.

The U.S. literacy rate had reached 90 percent by the beginning of the twentieth century, and soon it began to seem as if writing the "Great American Novel" had became the goal of every college-educated who was exposed to the writings of Dos Passos, Faulkner, Hemingway, and Steinbeck. Publishing and reading fiction would remain popular until television wrought its change on the American use of leisure time. By the 1940s, a new kind of paperback was creating a sensation: 25-cent "pocket" books sold on newsstands, at train and bus stations, as well as in book-stores. During World War II the government urged publishers to issue slimmed-down "pulp" (made from cheap paper) versions of books for the troops to carry with them.

By the 1950s, the boom in paperback sales had begun, and today the majority of books sold in the United States are softcover. By the 1970s, paperback reprints of the previous year's best-selling novels were setting publishing records, with title like Jaws, Shogun, and The Godfather selling as many as ten million copies—unheard of for a hardcover edition. Unit the 1960s, book publishing was a fairly stable industry, with large house headed by editors such as Bennett Cerf (Random House) and Ken McCormick (Doubleday). The editors, not the business people, decided what kinds of books would be published, and they worked with authors to nurture them. Of course book publishing was always a business, but the era of the great editors the myth persisted that the quest for literature was what drives book publishing. Today, publishers call the tune. Although the chairman of Simon & Schuster denied that corporate pressure from parent company Gull and Western, caused the cancellation of a particularly violent novel in 1990, the industry saw it as another indication of decisions of taste being decayed by the sensibilities of a conglomerate rather than an editor.

Hardcover or Paperback?

As a true mass market for paperbacks developed, publishers began to look at the financial success of the original hardcover edition. Sales of hardcover books dropped from 54 percent of sales in the late 1970s to less than half in the 1980s, with paperback sales increasing by a reciprocal amount, according to the nonprofit Book Industry Study Group. To counter the trend, publishers of hardback books selected sure-fire "blockbuster" books, printed them in large quantities, and then discounted them heavily, making them competitive with paperbacks.

Eventually the surging sales of paperbacks convinced publishers that many books were more appropriately publish in softcover. Many light entertainment and self-improvement books fall into this category today, along with the "instant books" that organizations with large staffs and resources such as Dell, Bantam, and The New York Times can assemble and print within days after an election, testimony before a congressional committee, a historic space flight, or the assassination of as leader. Many travel volumes, how-to books, humorous works, and cookbooks now originate as paperbacks.

In the 1980s, the publishers of novels by new writers and books aimed at younger adult readers—genres that are not usually very profitable—tried simultaneous publication of hardcover and softcover editions, with the paperback selling at about half the price of the hardback. Readers who prefer the more durable book have that option, but readers with less to spend on books need not wait a your for the cheaper version. The experiment met with considerable success: Paperback sales did not detract substantially from hardcover sales.

Best-selling hardback books are no longer the key to the market. Books, like the other print media, have became specialized. One customer enters a bookstore and goes directly to the "fitness" section. Another is interested in a genre such as romance, gothic, or horror fiction. Still another looks only for a new cookbook. Today's book mart is as complex as a major department store, thanks in part to the proliferation of the paperback.

The increased importance of the paperback has given rise to new jargon in the book publishing industry.

The "hard-soft deal" refers to the simultaneous acquisition of a book by a hardcover publisher and a softcover publisher, usually with the paperback publisher agreeing to market the book approximately a year after publication of the hardcover edition. Sometimes the two publishers are independent of one another, but increasingly they come under the same corporate umbrella, as with Simon & Schuster and Pocket Books, both units of Gulf & West ern.

"Trade paperbacks" are books published originally in paperback format, in a size larger than regular "mass-market," rack-size paperbacks, and at about half the price of a hardcover hook. While few major novelists have agreed to let their works begin as trade paperbacks, the format is becoming the leading choice for travel, diet, and cook books. The reason for the phenomenon is strictly economic: Consumers are more likely to spend $ 12.95 for a softcover book than $ 29.95 for a hardcover version.

Bookselling, like publishing, is dominated by financial concerns. To this day, some book stores make a profit by offering personalized service to individual customers. Oxford Square Books in Oxford, Mississippi, and the Elliot Bay Book Co. in Seattle are examples of independent bookstores that maintain a huge backlist (meaning books that have been in print for a year or more), which account for more than a third of their annual sales." Americans who shop mainly in malls are more familiar with Waldenbooks, B. Dalton, and Barnes & Noble (Dalton is now owned by Barnes &Noble). Dalton and Waldenbooks, with nearly 1000 units apiece, account for 35 to 40 percent of all books sold in the United States. Whereas the shopkeeper with the "book nook" and a small-town main street orders books by the ones and twos, Walden-books and Dalton order by the hundreds or thousands, keeping track of the in count it in order to create sales, or to "remainder" it at bargain price can have a great influence on whether it sells well. Chains place their stores in high-traffic urban and suburban shopping centres, and they promote and advertise heavily.

Publishers and authors may lament the clout the bookstore chains now wield, but at the same time they acknowledge that modern merchandising methods introduced by the chains have increased the sales of the most popular books. The large independent bookstores with their extensive backlist have managed to compute with chains by using computers to keep track of their titles.

Chains of bookstores are such a dominant force in the publishing industry today that they sometimes seem like elephants at the watering hole—shoving smaller creatures aside, if only in inadvertently because of their huge size. In 1988, the largest chain informed the smallest publishers that it would not handle their books unless these publishers distributed their product through a larger publisher or a wholesaler. For a large chain, dealing with tiny publishers simply isn't cost-efficient. Small publishers love the idea that getting their book in a chain guarantees 1000 outlets, but the chains find that more than half of the books from small publishers have to be returned unsold. At the beginning of the 1990s, Waldenbooks and B. Dalton were still adding outlets at the rate of 100 stores a bear. But the publishers, unhappy with many of the practices of the big chains, stopped giving them bigger discounts than the independent booksellers get. And competition from videos, Nintendo games, and other forms of electronic entertainment—along with soft economy of the early 1990s—suggests that the heyday of chain store growth may be nearly over.

Because textbooks and educational materials are enumerated in various categories by the Association of American Publishers (AAP), one might miss the point that college, elementary, and secondary texts (plus test materials and educational audiovisual items) account for nearly one-third the revenue of the publishing industry—greater than either trade books or professional books. Consider, too, that the category of "professional" book enumerated by the AAP includes volumes needed for continuing education. Textbooks, in short, are major category of book publishing.

Custom textbook publishing—assembling texts for individual course instructors by offering chapters and excerpts from many print sources— has grown in popularity, with photocopying firms leading the way in producing the texts. A 1991 decision against Kinko's for violating the Copyright Act has had the effect of clamping down on wholesale photocopying of protected materials. Book publishers, responding to the need for custom texts, have set up computerized operations that allow individual instructors to select from materials in a large database to request textbooks that reflect the material taught in their courses. Despite the passing of the baby boom that populated the school systems in the 1970s and 1980s, the textbook market is expected to continue as a major sector of American book publishing.

A few generations ago, the term literature and publishing might have been considered synonymous. Respected publishing houses led their lists with major novels from the nation's best-know writers. Biography, history, humor, inspirational works, cookbooks, and travel guides complemented the fiction.

As television filled the hours once devoted to reading, and as some writers turned to the more lucrative visual media, the novel waned in importance. The offerings from the book industry changed, catering to specific needs of narrow audiences. In the 1970s, Time magazine coined the term "nonbook" to refer to book like publications that sell in bookstores but focus on trivial or transient topics and are of questionable literary value

The New York Time Book Review used to publish two best-seller lists: fiction and nonfiction. In response to the way books are marketed today, the Time now publishes several best-seller lists in each week's Book Review section. Hardbacks and paperbacks are separated. "Advice, How-to and Miscellaneous" have their own list, separate from other nonfiction. With the sell-help categories and non-books removed, the nonfiction best-seller list is dominated by biographies of celebrates. In today's business environment, marketing is the word that has replaced literature in book publishing decisions. Publishers argue that hey will have the capital to publish worthwhile but unprofitable books for the elite public only if they successfully satisfy the needs of the masses who want sensational entertainment, help in flattening their abdomens, or schemes who want sensational entertainment, help in flattening their abdomens, or schemes for making millions quickly.

Let us look at an example of the impact of marketing mentality on contemporary publishing. The respected Boston publisher Little, Brown came out with Is Salami and Eggs Better Than Sex?, subtitled Memoirs of a Happy Eater. The book was by television and stage personality Alan King, and reviewers noted that he plundered many of his stand-up comedy routines fair the material in the book. A co-author was enlisted to flesh out the concept. She was Mimi Sheraton, former restaurant critic for The New York Times, who tossed off cutest introductions to each chapter and provided unusual recipes to end each chapter. In show business terminology, she was an "opening act" intended to build excitement for Mr. King's comic turn. The advertising for the book featured quotes from radio comedians Bob and Ray as well as singer Frank Sinatra, Whose quote "I have never known a couple who checked into a motel for salami and eggs" apparently provided the title for the book. Although these marketing ploys did help increase attention for the book from the mass media, none was sufficient to make the book a major success.

A few of the largest publishing houses still are known for their eclectic, well-rounded lists of books that cover the spectrum of interests. Doubleday and Random House are examples of such "general" publishers. The era of the general publisher is on the wane, however, and many houses prefer to specialize in an area where they can capture a large share of the market by limiting their expertise and building a reputation as having a strong list of titles. Specialization also help the publisher to train sales personnel, and to associate with the sales outlets that are best suited to its list of offerings.

Among the areas of specialized book publishing are these:

Reference—Directories, dictionaries, compendia of historical data, bibliographies. These expensive volumes are purchased manual by libraries, businesses, and specialists.

Professional—Knowledge esoteric to a specific field of business or trade, and directors or handbooks necessary for conduct of business. These often are sold through professional associations or by direct mail, as well as in retail outlets.

Textbooks—Designed to fit the specific needs and time frames of primary, secondary, and higher education. Sold to school systems and, in college, to individual students through campus bookstores.

Children's books—Picture books, early readers, science and learning, and juvenile fiction. Parents are the prime purchasers, and many children's books are purchased as gifts. Libraries also are as important market.

Technical, scientific, law, and medical—Volumes updating the specialized knowledge in fields were information about innovations must be disseminated rapidly.

Entertainment, self-improvement, how-to, religious, erotica, hobby—Works that cater to the special needs of the individual.

Of course this is only this is only a general and partial list. Some publishers handle mainly poetry, and others have a political slant. Moreover, each large publishing house day maintains several colophons (identifying symbols of individual printing houses) or divisions for the purpose of printing one or another of several specialized tapes of book. In other words, the big publishers want a chance to sell you precisely the kind of product that matches your needs and lift-style.

The author whose manuscript is rejected by every other publisher in the field need not forgo a literary career. Writer's Market, the guide for freelance writers, lists "subsidy book publishers" in a special section of its directory. There are at least a dozen, of which the best know is Vantage Press in New York. Known by the pejorative "vanity press" because they produce books for otherwise unpublished authors, the subsidy publishers require the author to pay for the entire venture. The books produced under this system may be perfectly competent in terms of physical production, but except for a single listing in a small ad, the publisher probably will not publicize the book. Vanity authors usually end up being their own best customers, although some vanity publishers can point to one or two books they've published that managed to find an audience and return the cost of production.

Market cells for innovation

How do you sell books? With a certain amount of daring and imagination:

- The Waldenbooks chain builds excitement, and "traffic," in its stores with displays of nonbook items: tape, calendars, and posters. The firm's chief executive advises publishers on the timing, design, and marketing of their books, and he sometimes reads manuscripts in order to help new authors.
- The Association of American Publishers has developed Pubnet, an electronic computerized book-ordering system, to help bookstores get stock quickly when there is consumer demand.
- The author of a novel mentioned specific products in her book...and then arranged for display featuring her book in fashionable stores (Such as Giorgio on Rodeo Drive in Beverly Hills) that sell the products she mentioned.
- Publishers of romance novels, popular with women, advise authors to alter the formula to include divorces and widowed heroines, reflecting the marital status of the consumers.
- One paperback publishing firm requires all its top editors, art directors, and other executives to take part in cover-selection meetings because its books are "impulse purchases," where the consumer makes up his or her mind to buy on the spot, with no influence other than personal reaction to the picture and the promotional "blurb" on the cover.

Studies indicate that only half of the reading-age public buys and reads books. "Heavy reader"—especially those age 25 to 44—account for a third of the reading population and 90 percent of general book sales. Mysteries are the most popular from of fiction, accounting for 17 percent of fiction sales. The top-selling nonfiction category is autobiography-biography."

The book industry used to experience the bulk of its sales in the autumn, leading up to the Christmas gift-giving season. That's still the leading period for sales of expensive gift books, and novels still sell well in the summer when people have more time to read. But book publishing less and less is seasonal, owing partly to the promotions of bookstore chains that want to promote books aggressively all year long and book clubs that want to offer attractive choices every month. Whereas January and February used to be shunned by publishers on the theory that few people bought books after the holidays, now those months are as likely to see a major book published as any other time of year.

Some books have a smooth, quick road to acceptance by a major publisher. The sports hero or movie star who decides to open a reminiscence, a fitness manual, or a cookbook usually can find an agent who will close the deal and arrange for a ghostwriter as well. Authors with proven track records usually develop a personal relationship with a senior editor at a major publishing house-someone proven in the business who can handle the ego and the special needs of major writer. Under such circumstances, publication is merely a matter of delivering a satisfactory manuscript; going through normal copy editing procedure stop check for grammar, style, and accuracy; and then waiting four of five months for typesetting, printing, binding, and delivery to the bookstores.

Such success stories are not representative of the process. More than 40,000 books are published in the

United States each year, but hundreds of thousand of unsolicited manuscripts—books written by new authors and submitted for consideration—float from author to agent to publisher and back. The agent, working on a commission from the author's earnings, works with authors to prepare manuscripts for submits in to publishers. Experienced writers normally prepare an outline or table of cements and a sample chapter, which they send to their agent or directly to an editor in hopes of getting encouragement.

Book editors must sift through these myriad submissions and proposals. They select the ones they feel have merit either on the basis of sales potential, "importance," or "fit" with the publisher's list for the next year. The editor then becomes an advocate for the manuscript within the publishing house and a devil's advocate with the author, arguing for larger production and advertising budgets on one hand and at the same time prodding the author to sharpen the content of the book to make it read better.

The production of most books takes a year or more to move from nearly completed manuscript to publication date. Memories, technical works, major novels, and yes, textbooks like this one, may take several years of work by the authors. Then the editorial, design, and marketing staffs must perform their skills. It can be a frustrating and lengthy but rewarding process.

New strategies for reaching readers

Book publishers once depended on publicity, good reviews, and favorable work of mouth to sell books. In the consumer-drives information market of the 1990s however, the book industry increasingly bases its decisions on what book buyers seem to want.

When a book like Norman Mailer's Harlot's Ghost costs $ 30 in hardbacks, for example, only the avid—and affluent—reader regularly buys hardback novels. Others have to depend on paperbacks. In order to broaden the market for hardbacks, publishers are experimenting with novels and biographies costing as little as $12.95. At that price, many readers accustomed to paying $3.95 for paperbacks and $7.95 for quality paperbacks are willing to make the move to hardbacks. The publisher has to control cost and publish a larger quantity at that price, but just as retailing shifted from the big old department stores to the discount stores, publishing may be shifting to those houses that can provide quality for less. In the age of television and USA Today, many readers don't want to spend two or three weeks plowing through a 500-page novel. That's why some publishers are encouraging their authors to aim for under 200 pages—the "quick read" that attracts busy readers.

Your boss tell you: "I read a great book on the plane back from Chicago. It's called The one-Minute Manager. Makes a lot of sense for anyone who wants to get ahead in business these day." On your pick up a copy The One-Minute Manager.

A friend asks: "Have you read the latest Dick Francis mystery? It's his best one yet...He really outdoes himself this time." The copy at the library is one a long waiting list, so you splurge on your own copy and plan to read it at the beach this weekend.

We've just described the two main reasons why people decide to buy new hardcover books: because the books have immediate and important utility, or because they'll keep you current with "what people are reading."

Sensational biographies of celebrities; history written by recent world leaders; mysteries set in exotic locales; novels that rip the curtain away from the world of entertainment, politics, or business; books that real new secrets of beauty, dieting, or fitness—these are some of the categories most likely to stimulate discussion among those who read.

Of course many books are bought and never read, because the urge to buy a book is often stronger then the urge to read a book. The term "coffeetable book" was coined in the 1960s to describe the oversized volumes, usually full of color photos, that are presented as gifts, especially at Christmas time. Coffeetable books display prints from art museums, recipes, travel photos, antique autos, architecture, or historical points of interest. They make impressive gifts.

Unread books also include many sell-improvement volumes, whose purchasers vainly hope to change their appearance, life-style, or success on the job, but for whom the urge to buy the book is stronger than the energy needed to read the book. Best-selling novels mentioned on television shows also may gather dust despite the good intentions of the buyer, who quickly forgets the reason for his or her enthusiasm over the subject.

Countless volumes of encyclopedias go unread, reference books remain unopened, art books gather dust, and instructional volumes await their first reading. All were purchased in the expectation that enlightenment would follow quickly, but the difficulty of finding time to read a book defeats the good intentions of many a book purchaser.

People often write their names in new books, reflecting the expectation that the content of the volume will have a deeply personal relevance and the book itself will remain a treasured possession. People often remember the names of the authors of the books they read.

Consider some of these observations about book buying and book reading as you explore the other print and electronic media described in the following chapters. All media have something in common but each medium is used in unique ways by each of us, according to our needs and orientation.

Believing literacy to be universal in the United States, publishers hardly expected to lose potential readership to the problem of illiteracy. But in urban America today, the school dropout problem and waves of immigrants from Third World countries have resulted in an alarming increase in nonreaders. Publishers are among many organisations striving to combat the problem through programs in schools and through community groups. In fact, materials to help tutor the illiterate are a new field of specialised publishing.

9

Publications and Public Relations

Dissemination of information on the progress made under the Indian space programme is given importance by the Department of Space to evoke public interest and support. All sections of the public including technical and scientific community, students and the general public are targeted under the publicity campaign. The public is informed of all major events through issue of press releases, holding press conferences, conduct of media tours, and providing video clippings. of major activities to the electronic media. Several exhibitions have been organised and technical and general literature on space activities published.

Media coverage

During the year the media including the electronic media has covered all important developments under the space programme. Several interviews to national and international journalists, including radio and television agencies have been given to bring out the technical achievements of the space programme. The space programme has received good coverage both in the national and international media.

Several radio talks have been given by scientists of DOS over All India Radio.

Exhibitions

Exhibitions play an important role in the publicity of

high technology programmes like space. Keeping this in view, DOS has arranged several exhibitions selecting the venues and occasions to attract maximum audience. During the year, DOS participated in the following exhibitions:

- Thrissur Pooram Exhibition organised by Thrissur Pooram Exhibition Committee at Thrissur in May 1998.
- AGRASAR- Exhibition in connection with the Golden Jubilee celebration of India's Independence at India Gate, New Delhi from August 3-16,1998.
- Exhibition at MES Teachers College, Bangalore, from September 1-3,1998.
- Broadcast Engineering Society Exhibition at Bangalore during September 25-26,1998.
- 3rd Indian Electrical Electronics & Telecommunications Fair ELCOM '98 at Bangalore during October 8-11,1998.
- Bangalore IT Com'98 during November 1-5, 1998.
- 14th National Convention of Electronics and Telecommunications Engineers at Guwahati during November 12-14,1998.
- CEOS Seminar at Bangalore during November 10-12,1998.
- Science Exhibition 1998-99 at New Horizon English High School, Bangalore, during November 14-16,1998.
- 2nd International High Energy Material Conference and Exhibition at IIT, Chennai during December 8-10,1998.

- Aero India - 98 Exhibition at Bangalore during December 8-12,1998.
- Indian Science Congress Exhibition at Chennai during January 3-10,1999.
- Aviation Exhibition at IIT, Mumbai during January 29-30,1999.
- ROTASTEX'99 Exhibition at Madurai during February 10-14,1999.

ISRO also sent displays to the exhibition organised by India Trade Promotion Organisation at Lisbon, Portugal during the year.

The Visveswaraya Industrial and Technological Museum, Bangalore, is being assisted by DOS for setting up a space gallery which is now in an advanced stage. Permanent exhibitions at VSSC, ISAC and SHAR were visited by a number of general public and by a large number of students during the Science Day celebration on February 28. DOS is also considering setting up of space museums in important cities.

Publications

Publicity materials including "India in Space" a leaflet in 12 languages besides English, stickers and posters on INSAT-2E, have been printed. Space India bringing out the progress under space programme have been brought out, both in Hindi and English. Space Spectrum a compilation of the progress in all aspects of space all over the world has also been brought out for restricted circulation within DOS to keep the scientists and engineers abreast of the latest developments in the field. Efforts are under way to publish popular books on space using private publishers. A book 'Jewels in the Sky' and a Kannada publication on INSAT have been brought out during the year. Two more books, 'Call of Space' and another on space science are in the pipeline. The publications brought out during the year are as follows:

1. Towards space-borne terrestrial imaging spectrometry (S K Srivastava, P P Nageswara Rao and V Jayaraman) (ISRO-NNRMS-SRû42-98)
2. Proceedings of the National Workshop on Material processing in space and space biotechnology (ISRO-SP-66-98)
3. Safety in handling cryogenics and briefs on some accidents and failures (ISRO-SP-67-98)
4. Library Profile, Policy and Procedure Manual (ISRO-SP-68-98)
5. An Atlas of North Indian Ocean Eddies from Topex Altimeter Derived Sea Surface Heights (ISRO-SP-69-98)
6. Safety in handling Liquid Propellants (ISRO-SP-70-98)
7. Item rate tender contract for works (provisional) (ISRO-CED-SP-71-98)
8. Flora of Sriharikota Island (ISRO-SHAR-TR-99-98)
9. Impact of ERS-1 scatterometer in Medium Range Forecasting / Cyclone and Monsoon (ISRO-SAC-SR-98-98)
10. Guidelines for non-destructive testing and evaluation: Ultrasonic (VSSC Publication)
11. NNRMS Bulletin -NNRMS-(B)-22,1998
12. IRS-1D Poster (Reprint)
13. Towards National Development (A Brochure in English and Hindi)
14. PSLV Brochure
15. APIB Booklet (in Kannada)

16. Brochure on Integrated Mission for Sustainable Development (for NRSA)
17. ISREL Newsletter, December 1998
18. INSAT-3A Leaflet
19. A book in Kannada entitled "Our Agricultural Resources - Our Plan": Agroclimatic Planning-Planning Commission (for Agroclimatic Regional Planning Unit, Ahmedabad)

General

In order to evoke interest among talented youngsters in science particularly in space, the first rank holders of X standard 1998 examination from all the States and Union Territories were invited to visit the space establishments during the year. Twenty students from different States and Union Territories participated in this fourteen day tour during which senior scientists briefed the students on the various activities. This is the second such tour organised; the first one had been organised last year.

In order to encourage talented youngsters to pursue science as their career, DOS is considering implementing a scheme of awarding scholarships to students taking up B.Sc and M.Sc courses. The details are being worked out.

The National Science Day was observed on February 28, 1999 at ISRO centres. The Centres allowed visitors on this day to the various facilities, conducted various competitions to school students and arranged special exhibitions and video shows. During the year VSSC and LPSC conducted various competitions to the students in which more than 20,000 students participated.

The information on the Indian Space Programme has also been made available on the Internet. This can be accessed at 'www.isro.org'.

10

Space in Parliament

Space programme continued to attract the attention of both Houses of Parliament during the year. In all, 36 questions were answered in Parliament during the year as follows:

	Lok Sabha	*Rajya Sabha*	*Total*
Starred	5	1	6
Unstarred	16	14	30
Total	21	15	36

The questions generally pertained to matters relating to launching of Geosynchronous Satellite Launch Vehicle, development of cryogenic engine, launching of INSAT satellites, India's role in global space market, satellite communication policy, launching of remote sensing satellites, satellite system utilisation, space plans for 9th Five Year Plan, etc.

A meeting of the Consultative Committee of the Parliament pertaining to Ministries of Planning and Programme Implementation, Science and Technology and Scientific Departments was held during the year.

The Department-related Parliament Standing Committee on Science & Technology, Environment and Forests held its meeting on June 26, 1998, to review the performance and considered the Demands for Grants of the Department for 1998-99. The Committee also visited some of the space centres during the year.

11

General

Progressive use of Hindi

Efforts towards implementation of progressive use of Hindi in DOS Centres have continued with vigour during this year also. The Official Language Implementation Committee (OLIC) of DOS held quarterly meetings to review the progress in the use of Hindi. National Mesosphere-Stratosphere Troposphere Radar Facility has been given representation in Departmental OLIC. The Central level OLIC has also been constituted in NMRF For effective implementation of Official Language Policy, a post of Hindi translator has been created in NMRF

The second Sub-Committee of the Committee of Parliament on Official Language reviewed the implementation of Official Language Policy at DOS Secretariat, Bangalore in January 1999.

Vikram Sarabhai Space Centre, Thiruvananthapuram, and Liquid Propulsion Systems Centre, Valiamala have won first and second prizes by Town OLIC respectively for progressive use of Hindi for the year 1997-98. An inter-centre seminar in Hindi on "SPACE-2000" was organised at ISTRAC, Bangalore, during December 1998 in which a number of scientists from DOS/ISRO Centres/Units participated and presented papers in Hindi. Hindi Day, Hindi Week and

Hindi Workshops have been organised during which competitions in essays, noting and drafting, typewriting, quiz, poetry recitation, debate etc., have been held. DOS organised the 12th Annual Hindi Essay writing/noting/drafting competition to encourage employees to use Hindi in their routine official work.

Training programme through Hindi teaching scheme and other arrangements have been strengthened. The percentage of employees possessing working knowledge of Hindi in DOS increased to more than 80 percent. Arrangements have been made for imparting training in Hindi typewriting in some Centres and the percentage of employees possessing knowledge of Hindi typewriting has increased considerably. As part of computerisation programme, bilingual software has been installed in personal computers in all Centres/Units of DOS/ISRO.

The ISRO quarterly, "'Space India", continued to be published in Hindi also. The Department's Annual Report, Performance Budget and the Detailed Demands for Grants are also brought out in Hindi. Annual Reports and the Audited Statements of Accounts of Antrix Corporation Limited, NMRF, PRL and NRSA have been brought out in bilingual form. A brochure on Indian Space Programme entitled "Towards National Development" has been brought out in Hindi also.

Housing

Housing for the personnel working in DOS has been receiving considerable attention. During the year, construction of additional quarters for LPSC at Nagercoil (99), SHAR Centre at Sriharikota (12) and SAC and PRL at Ahmedabad (64) have been completed. More quarters are under construction at Thiruvananthapuram (128) and Bangalore. The number of quarters that exists at present in different places is as follows:

Bangalore	1350
Hassan	269
Thiruvananthapuram (including Valiamala)	622
Aluva	30
Sriharikota	2611
Ahmedabad	671
Lucknow	39
Mahendragiri	124
Kharagpur	9
Port Blair	4
Total	5729

Medical facilities

The Contributory Health Service Scheme (CHSS) of the Department continued to be administered satisfactorily.

Educational facilities

DOS provides schooling facilities for the children of its employees at Sriharikota, Thiruvananthapuram, Bangalore and Ahmedabad. In Sriharikota and Thiruvananthapuram, DOS has set up Space Central Schools while DOS has cosponsored setting up of Kendriya Vidyalayas along with other institutions in Ahmedabad and Bangalore. All the schools have performed very well during the year obtaining good results in the public examinations.

Staff grievances redressal machinery

Staff Grievances Redressal Machinery as envisaged by the Government has been functioning satisfactorily in the Department. During the year under review 36 grievances were received by various Staff Grievances Committees under this Department. All of them have been disposed off.

Apprentice training

Training of apprentices in the technical and commercial trades, including graduate apprentices was continued in the Centres/Units of the Department as in the previous year. About 1197 apprentices were trained during the year and out of 742 successful apprentices, 11 were appointed on regular basis in various Centres/Units of the Department.

JCM

The scheme of Joint Consultative Machinery (JCM) of the Department of Space continued to function satisfactorily during the year, with constant interaction with the staff for amicable settlement of the issues involved. The twenty-fourth Meeting of the Departmental Council of JCM was held on August 22,1998. During the meeting various issues pertaining to the Service/Welfare of the employees were discussed.

Vigilance and disciplinary

The Department vigilance machinery continued its efforts to maintain proper vigilance on the space programme and to ensure expeditious finalisation of pending cases. Periodical review of pending cases has been undertaken. The status of cases disposed of during the year and those pending is as follows:

Recruitment of scheduled caste and scheduled tribe personnel

The Department continued its efforts to recruit qualified and eligible persons belonging to scheduled castes and scheduled tribes communities for appointment against posts reserved for them as per the Government orders on the subject.

	Gazetted Officers	*Others*
Brought forward from 1997	13	48

(Contd...)

Received during the year 1998	06	49
TOTAL	19	98
Disposed during the year 1998	02	40
Pending	17	58

Table-I indicates the status of recruitment of persons belonging to Scheduled Castes and Scheduled Tribes in the last two years and the year under report.

Recruitment of physically handicapped personnel

Appointment of Physically Handicapped persons, in accordance with the Policy of the Government and orders issued from time to time, has been continued.

Table-II indicates the status of representation of Physically Handicapped persons with reference to total employees.

Recruitment of ex-servicemen

The Department continued the special steps to implement the decision of the Government regarding rehabilitation and resettlement of ex-servicemen in civil posts, as per the orders of the Government.

Table-III indicates the status of representation of ex-servicemen with reference to the total number of employees in Group 'C' and 'D'.

Recruitment of other backward classes (OBCs)

Orders issued by the Department for reserving certain percentage of posts filled by direct recruitment for Other Backward Classes have been implemented in the Department and 114 persons belonging to Other Backward classes have been appointed by the Department so far.